The Garden of Kama

Complete Love Lyrics

Including
India's Love Lyrics
Stars of the Desert
Last Poems

By

Laurence Hope

With illustrations by Byam Shaw

DODD, MEAD & COMPANY
NEW YORK   1949

Copyright, 1902, 1905, 1906
By DODD, MEAD & COMPANY

Dedication to
MALCOLM NICOLSON

I, who of lighter love wrote many a verse,
  Made public never words inspired by thee,
Lest strangers' lips should carelessly rehearse
  Things that were sacred and too dear to me.

Thy soul was noble; through these fifteen years
  Mine eyes familiar, found no fleck nor flaw,
Stern to thyself, thy comrades' faults and fears
  Proved generosity thine only law.

Small joy was I to thee; before we met
  Sorrow had left thee all too sad to save.
Useless my love—as vain as this regret
  That pours my hopeless life across thy grave.

L. H.

Contents

	PAGE
"Less Than the Dust"	3
"To the Unattainable"	4
"In the Early, Pearly Morning": Song by Valgovind	5
Reverie of Mahomed Akram at the Tamarind Tank	7
Verses	12
Song of Khan Zada	13
The Teak Forest	14
Valgovind's Boat Song	18
Kashmiri Song by Juma	19
Zira: in Captivity	20
Marriage Thoughts: by Morsellin Khan	23
To the Unattainable: Lament of Mahomed Akram	26
Mahomed Akram's Appeal to the Stars	27
Reminiscence of Mahomed Akram	29
Story by Lalla-ji, the Priest	31
Request	33
Story of Udaipore: Told by Lalla-ji, the Priest	34
Valgovind's Song in the Spring	38
Youth	40
When Love Is Over: Song of Khan Zada	41
"Golden Eyes"	42

	PAGE
Kotri, by the River	45
Farewell	47
Afridi Love	48
Yasmini	52
Ojira, to Her Lover	56
Thoughts: Mahomed Akram	59
Prayer	60
The Aloe	62
Memory	63
The First Lover	66
Khan Zada's Song on the Hillside	68
Deserted Gipsy's Song: Hillside Camp	69
The Plains	71
"Lost Delight"—After the Hazara War	72
Unforgotten	75
Song of Faiz Ulla	77
Story of Lilavanti	78
The Garden by the Bridge	81
Fate Knows No Tears	85
Verses: Faiz Ulla	88
Two Songs by Sitara, of Kashmir	89
Second Song: The Girl from Baltistan	91
Palm Trees by the Sea	94
Song by Gulbaz	97
Kashmiri Song	99
Reverie of Ormuz the Persian	100
Sunstroke	103
Adoration	105

	PAGE
Three Songs of Zahir-u-Din	108
Second Song	110
Third Song, Written During Fever	112
The Regret of the Ranee in the Hall of Peacocks	114
Protest: By Zahir-u-Din	116
Famine Song	120
The Window Overlooking the Harbour	123
Back to the Border	126
Reverie: Zahir-u-Din	128
Sea Song	130
To the Hills!	132
Till I Wake	134
His Rubies: Told by Valgovind	135
Song of Taj Mahomed	139
The Garden of Kama: Kama the Indian Eros	140
Camp Follower's Song, Gomal River	142
Song of the Colours: by Taj Mahomed	145
Lalila, to the Ferengi Lover	149
On the City Wall	151
"Love Lightly"	153
No Rival Like the Past	155
Verse by Taj Mahomed	156
Lines by Taj Mahomed	157
There Is No Breeze to Cool the Heat of Love	158
Malay Song	162
The Temple Dancing Girl	164
Hira-Singh's Farewell to Burmah	166
Starlight	169

	PAGE
Sampan Song	170
Song of the Devoted Slave	171
The Singer	173
Malaria	175
Fancy	177
Feroza	178
This Month the Almonds Bloom at Kandahar	180

Stars of the Desert

To Aziz: Song of Mahomed Akram	185
Surf Song	186
Oh, Life, I Have Taken You for My Lover!	187
Illusion	190
Sleep	191
Song of the Enfifa River	193
The River of Pearls at Fez: Translation	196
Syed Amir	197
Au Salon	199
The Lute Player of Casa Blanca	200
The Hospital on the Shore	204
Among the Sandhills	205
The Cactus	206
Lalla Radha and the Churel	207
Rabat: Morocco	213
Gathered from Ternina's Face	215
Opium: Li's Riverside Hut at Taku	218
In the Water Palace	220
The Crucifix	226

	PAGE
Wind o' the Waste: On the Wall of Pekin	227
Happiness	228
The Orange Garden	230
Droit du Seigneur	232
Korean Song	238
Stars of the Desert	239
The Fisherman's Bride	241
The End	243
The Consolation of Dreams	247
Men Should Be Judged	249
The Island of Desolation: Song of Mahomed Akram	250
A Sea Pink	252
The Date-Garden	255
Trees of Wharncliffe House	258
All Farewells Should Be Gentle Spoken	262
Garden Song	264
The Match-Maker	266
Vain-Glory	268
Worth While	270
Invitation to the Jungle	271
The Sinjib Tree	273
The Outlaw	275
Return!	278
Philosophy of Morning	279
The Slave	283
The Seasons	285
Devotion of Aziz to Mir Khan	287
The Purple Dusk	295

	PAGE
Hamlili, the Sultan of Song	296
Love Is the Symbol of a Sacred Thing	298
Istar-i-Sahara	300
Love the Careless	303
Should Thou Consent	305
Reminiscence of Maeterlinck's "Life of the Bee"	307
On Deck	308
The Ocean Tramp	310
The Mirrored Stars of Tangier	311
At Simrole Tank	312
The Guru's Tale: the Enchanted Night	313
Among the Fuchsias	317
At the Taking of the Fort	318
Twilight	322
To Aziz	324
In the Vineyards	325
In the African Desert	326
The City: Song of Mahomed Akram	330
The Jungle Fear	332
Disloyal	334
The Court of Pomegranates	336
The Tower of Victory	340

Last Poems

The Masters	347
I Shall Forget	350
The Lament of Yasmini, the Dancing-Girl	351
Among the Rice Fields	356

	PAGE
The Bride	357
Unanswered	359
The Net of Memory	360
The Cactus Thicket	361
Song of the Peri	362
Though in My Firmament Thou Wilt Not Shine	364
The Convert	365
Ashore	367
Yasin Khan	368
Khristna and His Flute	371
Song of Jasoda	373
Song of Ramesram Temple Girl	376
The Rao of Ilore	378
To M. C. N.	380
Disappointment	381
On Pilgrimage	384
The Rice-Boat	385
Lallji, My Desire	388
Rutland Gate	390
Atavism	391
Middle-Age	392
The Jungle Flower	394
From Behind the Lattice	395
Wings	396
Song of the Parao (Camping-Ground)	397
The Tom-Toms	401
Written in Cananore	403
Feroke	405

	PAGE
My Desire	406
Sher Afzul	408
Nay, Not To-night	412
The Dying Prince	414
The Hut	417
My Paramour Was Loneliness	418
The Rice Was Under Water	419
"Surface Rights"	420
Shivratri (the Night of Shiva)	423
The First Wife	425
I Arise and Go Down to the River	428
Listen, Beloved	432
Oh, Unforgotten and Only Lover	436
Early Love	441
Vayu the Wind	444

Illustrations

The Garden of Kama	*Frontispiece*

FACING PAGE

Zira: In Captivity	20
Afridi Love	48
The Temple Dancing Girl	164
Feroza	178
Love is the Symbol of a Sacred Thing	298
Lallji, My Desire	388
I Arise and Go Down to the River	428

India's Love Lyrics

India's Love Lyrics

"Less than the Dust"

Less than the dust, beneath thy Chariot wheel,
Less than the rust, that never stained thy Sword,
Less than the trust thou hast in me, O Lord,
     Even less than these!

Less than the weed, that grows beside thy door,
Less than the speed of hours spent far from thee,
Less than the need thou hast in life of me.
     Even less am I.

Since I, O Lord, am nothing unto thee,
See here thy Sword, I make it keen and bright,
Love's last reward, Death, comes to me to-night,
     Farewell, Zahir-u-din.

"To the Unattainable"

OH, that my blood were water, thou athirst,
And thou and I in some far Desert land,
How would I shed it gladly, if but first
It touched thy lips, before it reached the sand.

Once,—ah, the Gods were good to me,—I threw
Myself upon a poison snake, that crept
Where my Beloved—a lesser love we knew
Than this which now consumes me wholly—slept.

But thou; alas, what can I do for thee?
By Fate, and thine own beauty, set above
The need of all or any aid from me,
Too high for service, as too far for love.

"In the Early, Pearly Morning":
Song by Valgovind

THE fields are full of Poppies, and the skies are very blue,
By the Temple in the coppice, I wait, Beloved, for you.
The level land is sunny, and the errant air is gay,
With the scent of rose and honey; will you come to me
to-day?

From carven walls above me, smile lovers; many a pair.
"Oh, take this rose and love me!" She has twined it in her
hair.
He advances, she retreating, pursues and holds her fast,
The sculptor left them meeting, in a close embrace at last.

Through centuries together, in the carven stone they lie,
In the glow of golden weather, and endless azure sky.
Oh, that we, who have for pleasure so short and scant a stay,
Should waste our summer leisure; will you come to me
to-day?

The Temple bells are ringing, for the marriage month has
come.

I hear the women singing, and the throbbing of the drum.
And when the song is failing, or the drums a moment mute,
The weirdly wistful wailing of the melancholy flute.

Little life has got to offer, and little man to lose,
Since to-day Fate deigns to proffer, oh wherefore, then,
                                                    refuse
To take this transient hour, in the dusky Temple gloom
While the poppies are in flower, and the mangoe trees
                                                    abloom.

And if Fate remember later, and come to claim her due,
What sorrow will be greater than the Joy I had with you?
For to-day, lit by your laughter, between the crushing
                                                    years,
I will chance, in the hereafter, eternities of tears.

Reverie of Mahomed Akram at the Tamarind Tank

The Desert is parched in the burning sun
And the grass is scorched and white.
But the sand is passed, and the march is done,
We are camping here to-night.
     I sit in the shade of the Temple walls,
     While the cadenced water evenly falls,
     And a peacock out of the Jungle calls
     To another, on yonder tomb.
    Above, half seen, in the lofty gloom,
    Strange works of a long dead people loom,
Obscene and savage and half effaced—
An elephant hunt, a musicians' feast—
And curious matings of man and beast;
What did they mean to the men who are long since dust?
    Whose fingers traced,
    In this arid waste,
These rioting, twisted, figures of love and lust?

Strange, weird things that no man may say,
Things Humanity hides away;—
    Secretly done,—

Catch the light of the living day,
    Smile in the sun.
Cruel things that man may not name,
Naked here, without fear or shame,
    Laughed in the carven stone.

Deep in the Temple's innermost Shrine is set,
    Where the bats and shadows dwell,
The worn and ancient Symbol of Life, at rest
    In its oval shell,
By which the men, who, of old, the land possessed,
Represented their Great Destroying Power.
    I cannot forget
That, just as my life was touching its fullest flower,
Love came and destroyed it all in a single hour,
    Therefore the dual Mystery suits me well.

    Sitting alone,
The tank's deep water is cool and sweet,
Soothing and fresh to the wayworn feet,
    Dreaming, under the Tamarind shade,
    One silently thanks the men who made
So green a place in this bitter land
    Of sunburnt sand.

The peacocks scream and the grey Doves coo,
Little green, talkative Parrots woo,
And small grey Squirrels, with fear askance,
At alien me, in their furtive glance,

Come shyly, with quivering fur, to see
The stranger under their Tamarind tree.

      Daylight dies,
The Camp fires redden like angry eyes,
      The Tents show white,
      In the glimmering light,
Spirals of tremulous smoke arise, to the purple skies,
   And the hum of the Camp sounds like the sea,
   Drifting over the sand to me.
      Afar, in the Desert some wild voice sings
        To a jangling zither with minor strings,
        And, under the stars growing keen above,
        I think of the thing that I love.

  A beautiful thing, alert, serene,
With passionate, dreaming, wistful eyes,
Dark and deep as mysterious skies,
Seen from a vessel at sea.
Alas, you drifted away from me,
And Time and Space have rushed in between,
But they cannot undo the Thing-that-has-been,
      Though it never again may be.
You were mine, from dusk until dawning light,
For the perfect whole of that bygone night
      You belonged to me!

They say that Love is a light thing,
A foolish thing and a slight thing,

A ripe fruit, rotten at core;
They speak in this futile fashion
To me, who am wracked with passion,
Tormented beyond compassion,
    For ever and ever more.

They say that Possession lessens a lover's delight,
  As radiant mornings fade into afternoon.
I held what I loved in my arms for many a night,
  Yet ever the morning lightened the sky too soon.

Beyond our tents the sands stretch level and far,
Around this little oasis of Tamarind trees.
A curious, Eastern fragrance fills the breeze
From the ruinous Temple garden where roses are.

I dream of the rose-like perfume that fills your hair,
Of times when my lips were free of your soft closed eyes,
While down in the tank the waters ripple and rise
And the flying foxes silently cleave the air.

The present is subtly welded into the past,
My love of you with the purple Indian dusk,
With its clinging scent of sandal incense and musk,
    And withering jasmin flowers.
My eyes grow dim and my senses fail at last,
    While the lonely hours
Follow each other, silently, one by one,
    Till the night is almost done.

Then weary, and drunk with dreams, with my garments damp
And heavy with dew, I wander towards the camp.
   Tired, with a brain in which fancy and fact are blent,
   I stumble across the ropes till I reach my tent
And then to rest. To ensweeten my sleep with lies,
To dream I lie in the light of your long lost eyes,
         My lips set free,
To love and linger over your soft loose hair—
To dream I lay your delicate beauty bare
         To solace my fevered eyes.
Ah,—if my life might end in a night like this—
Drift into death from dreams of your granted kiss!

Verses

You are my God, and I would fain adore You
    With sweet and secret rites of other days.
Burn scented oil in silver lamps before You,
    Pour perfume on Your feet with prayer and praise.

Yet are we one; Your gracious condescension
    Granted, and grants, the loveliness I crave.
One, in the perfect sense of Eastern mention,
    "Gold and the Bracelet, Water and the Wave."

Song of Khan Zada

As one may sip a Stranger's Bowl
You gave yourself but not your soul.
I wonder, now that time has passed,
Where you will come to rest at last.

You gave your beauty for an hour,
I held it gently as a flower,
You wished to leave me, told me so,—
I kissed your feet and let you go.

The Teak Forest

WHETHER I loved you who shall say?
Whether I drifted down your way
In the endless River of Chance and Change,
And you woke the strange
Unknown longings that have no names,
But burn us all in their hidden flames,
        Who shall say?

Life is a strange and a wayward thing:
We heard the bells of the Temples ring,
The married children, in passing, sing.
The month of marriage, the month of spring,
Was full of the breath of sunburnt flowers
That bloom in a fiercer light than ours,
And, under a sky more fiercely blue,
        I came to you!

You told me tales of your vivid life
Where death was cruel and danger rife—
Of deep dark forests, of poisoned trees,
Of pains and passions that scorch and freeze,
Of southern noontides and eastern nights,
Where love grew frantic with strange delights,

While men were slaying and maidens danced,
Till I, who listened, lay still, entranced.
Then, swift as a swallow heading south,
    I kissed your mouth!

One night when the plains were bathed in blood
From sunset light in a crimson flood,
We wandered under the young teak trees
Whose branches whined in the light night breeze;
You led me down to the water's brink,
"The Spring where the Panthers come to drink
At night; there is always water here
Be the season never so parched and sere."
Have we souls of beasts in the forms of men?
I fain would have tasted your life-blood then.

The night fell swiftly; this sudden land
Can never lend us a twilight strand
'Twixt the daylight shore and the ocean night,
But takes—as it gives—at once, the light.
We laid us down on the steep hillside,
While far below us wild peacocks cried,
And we sometimes heard, in the sunburnt grass,
The stealthy steps of the Jungle pass.
We listened; knew not whether they went
On love or hunger the more intent.
And under your kisses I hardly knew
Whether I loved or hated you.

But your words were flame and your kisses fire,
And who shall resist a strong desire?
Not I, whose life is a broken boat
On a sea of passions, adrift, afloat.
And, whether I came in love or hate,
That I came to you was written by Fate
In every hue of the blood-red sky,
In every tone of the peacocks' cry.

While every gust of the Jungle night
Was fanning the flame you had set alight.
For these things have power to stir the blood
And compel us all to their own chance mood.
And to love or not we are no more free
Than a ripple to rise and leave the sea.

We are ever and always slaves of these,
Of the suns that scorch and the winds that freeze,
Of the faint sweet scents of the sultry air,
Of the half heard howl from the far off lair.
These chance things master us ever. Compel
To the heights of Heaven, the depths of Hell.

Whether I love you? You do not ask,
Nor waste yourself on the thankless task.
I give your kisses at least return,
What matter whether they freeze or burn.
I feel the strength of your fervent arms,
What matter whether it heals or harms.

You are wise; you take what the Gods have sent.
You ask no question, but rest content
So I am with you to take your kiss,
And perhaps I value you more for this.
For this is Wisdom; to love, to live,
To take what Fate, or the Gods, may give,
To ask no question, to make no prayer,
To kiss the lips and caress the hair,
Speed passion's ebb as you greet its flow,—
To have,—to hold,—and,—in time,—let go!

And this is our Wisdom: we rest together
On the great lone hills in the storm-filled weather,
And watch the skies as they pale and burn,
The golden stars in their orbits turn,
While Love is with us, and Time and Peace,
And life has nothing to give but these.
But, whether you love me, who shall say,
Or whether you, drifting down my way
In the great sad River of Chance and Change,
With your looks so weary and words so strange,
Lit my soul from some hidden flame
To a passionate longing without a name,
      Who shall say?
Not I, who am but a broken boat,
Content for a while to drift afloat
In the little noontide of love's delights
      Between two Nights.

Valgovind's Boat Song

WATERS glisten and sunbeams quiver,
        The wind blows fresh and free.
Take my boat to your breast, O River!
        Carry me out to Sea!

This land is laden with fruit and grain,
        With never a place left free for flowers,
A fruitful mother; but I am fain
        For brides in their early bridal hours.

Take my boat to your breast, O River!
        Carry me out to Sea!

The Sea, beloved by a thousand ships,
        Is maiden ever, and fresh and free.
Ah, for the touch of her cool green lips,
        Carry me out to Sea!

Take my boat to your breast, dear River,
        And carry it out to Sea!

Kashmiri Song by Juma

You never loved me, and yet to save me,
One unforgettable night you gave me
Such chill embraces as the snow-covered heights
Receive from clouds, in northern, Auroral nights.
Such keen communion as the frozen mere
Has with immaculate moonlight, cold and clear.
And all desire,
Like failing fire,
Died slowly, faded surely, and sank to rest
Against the delicate chillness of your breast.

Zira: in Captivity

Love me a little, Lord, or let me go,
I am so weary walking to and fro
Through all your lonely halls that were so sweet
Did they but echo to your coming feet.

When by the flowered scrolls of lace-like stone—
Our women's windows—I am left alone,
Across the yellow Desert, looking forth,
I see the purple hills towards the north.

Behind those jagged Mountains' lilac crest
Once lay the captive bird's small rifled nest.
There was my brother slain, my sister bound;
His blood, her tears, drunk by the thirsty ground.

Then, while the burning village smoked on high,
And desecrated all the peaceful sky,
They took us captive, us, born frank and free,
On fleet, strong camels through the sandy sea.

Yet, when we rested, night-times, on the sand
By the rare waters of this dreary land,
Our captors, ere the camp was wrapped in sleep,
Talked, and I listened, and forgot to weep.

Zira: In Captivity

"Is he not brave and fair?" they asked, "our King,
Slender as one tall palm-tree by a spring;
Erect, serene, with gravely brilliant eyes,
As deeply dark as are these desert skies.

"Truly no bitter fate," they said, and smiled,
"Awaits the beauty of this captured child!"
Then something in my heart began to sing,
And secretly I longed to see the King.

Sometimes the other maidens sat in tears,
Sometimes, consoled, they jested at their fears,
Musing what lovers Time to them would bring;
But I was silent, thinking of the King.

Till, when the weary endless sands were passed.
When, far to south, the city rose at last,
All speech forsook me and my eyelids fell,
Since I already loved my Lord so well.

Then the division: some were sent away
To merchants in the city; some, they say,
To summer palaces, beyond the walls.
But me they took straight to the Sultan's halls.

Every morning I would wake and say
"Ah, sisters, shall I see our Lord to-day?"
The women robed me, perfumed me, and smiled;
"When were his feet unfleet to pleasure, child?"

And tales they told me of his deeds in war,
Of how his name was reverenced afar;
And, crouching closer in the lamp's faint glow,
They told me of his beauty, speaking low.

What need, what need? the women wasted art;
I love you with every fibre of my heart
Already. My God! when did I *not* love you,
In life, in death, when shall I not love you?

You never seek me. All day long I lie
Watching the changes of the far-off sky
Behind the lattice-work of carven stone.
And all night long, alas! I lie alone.

But you come never. Ah, my Lord the King,
How can you find it well to do this thing?
Come once, come only: sometimes, as I lie,
I doubt if I shall see you first, or die.

Ah, could I hear your footsteps at the door
Hallow the lintel and caress the floor,
Then I might drink your beauty, satisfied,
Die of delight, ere you could reach my side.

Alas, you come not, Lord: life's flame burns low,
Faint for a loveliness it may not know,
Faint for your face, oh, come—come soon to me—
Lest, though you should not, Death should, set me free.

Marriage Thoughts:
by Morsellin Khan

Bridegroom

    I give you my house and my lands, all golden with harvest;
    My sword, my shield, and my jewels, the spoils of my strife,
    My strength and my dreams, and aught I have gathered of glory,
    And to-night—to-night, I shall give you my very life.

Bride

    I may not raise my eyes, O my Lord, towards you,
    And I may not speak: what matter? my voice would fail.
    But through my downcast lashes, feeling your beauty,
    I shiver and burn with pleasure beneath my veil.

Younger Sisters

    We throw sweet perfume upon her head,
    And delicate flowers round her bed.
    Ah, would that it were our turn to wed!

Mother
>I see my daughter, vaguely, through my tears,
>(Ah, lost caresses of my early years!)
>I see the bridegroom, King of men in truth!
>(Ah, my first lover, and my vanished youth!)

Bride
>Almost I dread this night. My senses fail me.
>How shall I dare to clasp a thing so dear?
>Many have feared your name, but I your beauty.
>Lord of my life, be gentle to my fear!

Younger Sisters
>In the softest silk is our sister dressed,
>With silver rubies upon her breast,
>Where a dearer treasure to-night will rest.

Dancing Girls
>See! his hair is like silk, and his teeth are whiter
>Than whitest of jasmin flowers. Pity they marry him thus.
>I would change my jewels against his caresses.
>Verily, sisters, this marriage is greatly a loss to us!

Bride
>Would that the music ceased and the night drew round us,

With solitude, shadow, and sound of closing doors,
So that our lips might meet and our beings mingle,
While mine drank deep of the essence, beloved, of
yours

Passing Mendicant
    Out of the joy of your marriage feast,
        Oh, brothers, be good to me.
    The way is long and the Shrine is far,
        Where my weary feet would be.

    And feasting is always somewhat sad
        To those outside the door—
    Still; Love is only a dream, and **Life**
        Itself is hardly more!

To the Unattainable:
Lament of Mahomed Akram

I WOULD have taken Golden Stars from the sky for your necklace,
I would have shaken rose-leaves for your rest from all the rose-trees.

But you had no need; the short sweet grass sufficed for your slumber,
And you took no heed of such trifles as gold or a necklace.

There is an hour, at twilight, too heavy with memory.
There is a flower that I fear, for your hair had its fragrance.

I would have squandered Youth for you, and its hope and its promise,
Before you wandered, careless, away from my useless passion.

But what is the use of my speech, since I know of no words to recall you?
I am praying that Time may teach, you, your Cruelty, me, Forgetfulness.

Mahomed Akram's Appeal to the Stars

Oh, Silver Stars that shine on what I love,
  Touch the soft hair and sparkle in the eyes,—
Send, from your calm serenity above,
  Sleep to whom, sleepless, here, despairing lies.

Broken, forlorn, upon the Desert sand
  That sucks these tears, and utterly abased,
Looking across the lonely, level land,
  With thoughts more desolate than any waste.

Planets that shine on what I so adore,
  Now thrown, the hour is late, in careless rest,
Protect that sleep, which I may watch no more,
  I, the cast out, dismissed and dispossessed.

Far in the hillside camp, in slumber lies
  What my worn eyes worship but never see.
Happier Stars! your myriad silver eyes
  Feast on the quiet face denied to me.

Loved with a love beyond all words or sense,
    Lost with a grief beyond the saltest tear,
So lovely, so removed, remote, and hence
    So doubly and so desperately dear!

Stars! from your skies so purple and so calm,
    That through the centuries your secrets keep,
Send to this worn-out brain some Occult Balm,
    Send me, for many nights so sleepless, sleep.

And ere the sunshine of the Desert jars
    My sense with sorrow and another day,
Through your soft Magic, oh, my Silver Stars!
    Turn sleep to Death in some mysterious way.

Reminiscence of Mahomed Akram

I shall never forget you, never. Never escape
Your memory woven about the beautiful things of life.

The sudden Thought of your Face is like a Wound
            When it comes unsought
On some scent of Jasmin, Lilies, or pale Tuberose.
Any one of the sweet white fragrant flowers,
Flowers I used to love and lay in your hair.

Sunset is terribly sad. I saw you stand
Tall against the red and the gold like a slender palm;
The light wind stirred your hair as you waved your hand,
Waved farewell, as ever, serene and calm,
To me, the passion-wearied and tossed and torn,
Riding down the road in the gathering grey.
            Since that day
The sunset red is empty, the gold forlorn.

Often across the Banqueting board at nights
Men linger about your name in careless praise,
The name that cuts deep into my soul like a knife;
And the gay guest-faces and flowers and leaves and lights

Fade away from the failing sense in a haze,
        And the music sways
Far away in unmeasured distance. . . .
        I cannot forget—
I cannot escape. What are the Stars to me?
Stars that meant so much, too much, in my youth;
Stars that sparkled about your eyes,
Made a radiance round your hair,
        What are they now?

Lingering lights of a Finished Feast,
Little lingering sparks rather,
    Of a Light that is long gone out.

Story by Lalla-ji, the Priest

He loved the Plant with a keen delight,
    A passionate fervour, strange to see,
Tended it ardently, day and night,
    Yet never a flower lit up the tree.

The leaves were succulent, thick, and green,
    And, sessile, out of the snakelike stem
Rose spine-like fingers, alert and keen,
    To catch at aught that molested them.

But though they nurtured it day and night,
    With love and labour, the child and he
Were never granted the longed-for sight
    Of a flower crowning the twisted tree.

Until one evening a wayworn Priest
    Stopped for the night in the Temple shade
And shared the fare of their simple feast
    Under the vines and the jasmin laid.

He, later, wandering round the flowers
    Paused awhile by the blossomless tree.

The man said, "May it be fault of ours,
　　That never its buds my eyes may see?

"Aslip it came from the further East
　　Many a sunlit summer ago."
"It grows in our Jungles," said the Priest,
　　"Men see it rarely; but this I know,

"The Jungle people worship it; say
　　They bury a child around its roots—
Bury it living;—the only way
　　To crimson glory of flowers and fruits."

He spoke in whispers; his furtive glance
　　Probing the depths of the garden shade.
The man came closer, with eyes askance,
　　The child beside them shivered, afraid.

A cold wind drifted about the three,
　　Jarring the spines with a hungry sound,
The spines that grew on the snakelike tree
　　And guarded its roots beneath the ground.

　　　　.　.　.　.　.　.

After the fall of the summer rain
　　The plant was glorious, redly gay,
Blood-red with blossom. Never again
　　Men saw the child in the Temple play.

Request

Give me yourself one hour; I do not crave
    For any love, or even thought, of me.
Come, as a Sultan may caress a slave
    And then forget for ever, utterly.

Come! as west winds, that passing, cool and wet,
    O'er desert places, leave them fields in flower
And all my life, for I shall not forget,
    Will keep the fragrance of that perfect hour!

Story of Udaipore: Told by Lalla-ji, the Priest

"And when the Summer Heat is great,
   And every hour intense,
The Moghra, with its subtle flowers,
   Intoxicates the sense."

The Coco palms stood tall and slim, against the golden-glow,
And all their grey and graceful plumes were waving to and fro.

She lay forgetful in the boat, and watched the dying Sun
Sink slowly lakewards, while the stars replaced him, one by one.

She saw the marble Temple walls long white reflections make,
The echoes of their silvery bells were thrown across the lake.

The evening air was very sweet; from off the island bowers
Came scents of Moghra trees in bloom, and Oleander flowers.

> "The Moghra flowers that smell so sweet
> When love's young fancies play;
> The acrid Moghra flowers, still sweet
> Though love be burnt away."

The boat went drifting, uncontrolled, the rower rowed no more,
But deftly turned the slender prow towards the further shore.

The dying sunset touched with gold the Jasmin in his hair;
His eyes were darkly luminous: she looked and found him fair.

And so persuasively he spoke, she could not say him nay,
And when his young hands took her own, she smiled and let them stay.

And all the youth awoke in him, all love of Love in her,
All scents of white and subtle flowers that filled the twilight air

Combined together with the night in kind conspiracy
To do Love service, while the boat went drifting onwards, free.

> "The Moghra flowers, the Moghra flowers,
> While Youth's quick pulses play

> They are so sweet, they still are sweet,
> Though passion burns away."

Low in the boat the lovers lay, and from his sable curls
The Jasmin flowers slipped away to rest among the girl's.

Oh, silver lake and silver night and tender silver sky!
Where as the hours passed, the moon rose white and cold on high.

> "The Moghra flowers, the Moghra flowers,
> So dear to Youth at play;
> The small and subtle Moghra flowers
> That only last a day."

Suddenly, frightened, she awoke, and waking vaguely saw
The boat had stranded in the sedge that fringed the further shore.

The breeze grown chilly, swayed the palms; she heard, still half awake,
A prowling jackal's hungry cry blown faintly o'er the lake.

She shivered, but she turned to kiss his soft, remembered face,
Lit by the pallid light he lay, in Youth's abandoned grace.

But as her lips met his she paused, in terror and dismay,
The white moon showed her by her side asleep a Leper lay.

"Ah, Moghra flowers, white Moghra flowers,
   All love is blind, they say;
The Moghra flowers, so sweet, so sweet,
   Though love be burnt away!"

Valgovind's Song in the Spring

The Temple bells are ringing,
The young green corn is springing,
    And the marriage month is drawing very near.
I lie hidden in the grass,
And I count the moments pass,
    For the month of marriages is drawing near.

Soon, ah, soon, the women spread
The appointed bridal bed
    With hibiscus buds and crimson marriage flowers,
Where, when all the songs are done,
And the dear dark night begun,
    I shall hold her in my happy arms for hours.

She is young and very sweet,
From the silver on her feet
    To the silver and the flowers in her hair,
And her beauty makes me swoon,
As the Moghra trees at noon
    Intoxicate the hot and quivering air.

Ah, I would the hours were fleet
As her silver circled feet,
> I am weary of the daytime and the night;
I am weary unto death,
Oh my rose with jasmin breath,
> With this longing for your beauty and your light.

Youth

I am not sure if I knew the truth
   What his case or crime might be,
I only know that he pleaded Youth,
   A beautiful, golden plea!

Youth, with its sunlit, passionate eyes,
   Its roseate velvet skin—
A plea to cancel a thousand lies,
   Or a thousand nights of sin.

The men who judged him were old and grey,
   Their eyes and their senses dim,
He brought the light of a warm Spring day
   To the Court-house bare and grim.

Could he plead guilty in a lovelier way?
His judges acquitted him.

When Love Is Over: Song of Khan Zada

Only in August my heart was aflame,
   Catching the scent of your Wind-stirred hair,
Now, though you spread it to soften my sleep
   Through the night, I should hardly care.

Only last August I drank that water
   Because it had chanced to cool your hands;
When love is over, how little of love
   Even the lover understands!

"Golden Eyes"

Oh Amber Eyes, oh Golden Eyes!
    Oh Eyes so softly gay!
Wherein swift fancies fall and rise,
    Grow dark and fade away.
Eyes like a little limpid pool
    That holds a sunset sky,
While on its surface, calm and cool,
    Blue water lilies lie.

Oh Tender Eyes, oh Wistful Eyes,
    You smiled on me one day,
And all my life, in glad surprise,
    Leapt up and pleaded "Stay!"
Alas, oh cruel, starlike eyes,
    So grave and yet so gay,
You went to lighten other skies,
    Smiled once and passed away.

Oh, you whom I name "Golden Eyes,"
    Perhaps I used to know
Your beauty under other skies
    In lives lived long ago.

Perhaps I rowed with galley slaves
   Whose labour never ceased,
To bring across Phœnician waves
   Your treasure from the East.

Maybe you were an Emperor then
   And I a favourite slave;
Some youth, whom from the lions' den
   You vainly tried to save!
Maybe I reigned, a mighty King,
   The early nations knew,
And you were some slight captive thing,
   Some maiden whom I slew.

Perhaps, adrift on desert shores
   Beside some shipwrecked prow,
I gladly gave my life for yours.
   Would I might give it now!
Or on some sacrificial stone
   Strange Gods we satisfied,
Perhaps you stooped and left a throne
   To kiss me ere I died.

Perhaps, still further back than this,
   In times ere men were men,
You granted me a moment's bliss
   In some dark desert den,
When, with your amber eyes alight
   With iridescent flame,

And fierce desire for love's delight,
  Towards my lair you came.

Ah laughing, ever-brilliant eyes,
  These things men may not know,
But something in your radiance lies,
  That, centuries ago,
Lit up my life in one wild blaze
  Of infinite desire
To revel in your golden rays,
  Or in your light expire.

If this, oh Strange Ringed Eyes, be true,
  That through all changing lives
This longing love I have for you
  Eternally survives,
May I not sometimes dare to dream
  In some far time to be
Your softly golden eyes may gleam
  Responsively on me?

Ah gentle, subtly changing eyes,
  You smiled on me one day,
And all my life in glad surprise
  Leaped up, imploring "Stay!"
Alas, alas, oh Golden Eyes,
  So cruel and so gay,
You went to shine in other skies,
  Smiled once and passed **away.**

Kotri, by the River

At Kotri, by the river, when the evening's sun is low,
The waving palm trees quiver, the golden waters glow,
The shining ripples shiver, descending to the sea;
At Kotri, by the river, she used to wait for me.

So young, she was, and slender, so pale with wistful eyes
As luminous and tender as Kotri's twilight skies.
Her face broke into flowers, red flowers at the mouth,
Her voice,—she sang for hours like bulbuls in the south.

We sat beside the water through burning summer days,
And many things I taught her of Life and all its ways,
Of Love, man's loveliest duty, of Passion's reckless pain,
Of Youth, whose transient beauty comes once, but not
again.

She lay and laughed and listened beside the water's edge.
The glancing river glistened and glinted through the sedge.
Green parrots flew above her and, as the daylight died,
Her young arms drew her lover more closely to her side.

Oh days so warm and golden! oh nights so cool and still!
When Love would not be holden, and Pleasure had his will.

Days, when in after leisure, content to rest we lay,
Nights, when her lips' soft pressure drained all my life away.

And while we sat together, beneath the Babul trees,
The fragrant, sultry weather cooled by the river breeze,
If passion faltered ever, and left the senses free,
We heard the tireless river descending to the sea.

I know not where she wandered, or went in after days,
Or if her youth she squandered in Love's more doubtful
                                                                    ways.
Perhaps, beside the river, she died, still young and fair;
Perchance the grasses quiver above her slumber there.

At Kotri, by the river, maybe I too shall sleep
The sleep that lasts for ever, too deep for dreams; too deep.
Maybe among the shingle and sand of floods to be
Her dust and mine may mingle and float away to sea.

Ah Kotri, by the river, when evening's sun is low,
Your faint reflections quiver, your golden ripples glow.
You knew, oh Kotri river, that love which could not last.
For me your palms still shiver with passions of the past.

Farewell

Farewell, Aziz, it was not mine to fold you
    Against my heart for any length of days.
I had no loveliness, alas, to hold you,
    No siren voice, no charm that lovers praise.

Yet, in the midst of grief and desolation,
    Solace I my despairing soul with this:
Once, for my life's eternal consolation,
    You lent my lips your loveliness to kiss.

Ah, that one night! I think Love's very essence
    Distilled itself from out my joy and pain,
Like tropical trees, whose fervid inflorescence
    Glows, gleams, and dies, never to bloom again.

Often I marvel how I met the morning
    With living eyes after that night with you,
Ah, how I cursed the wan, white light for dawning,
    And mourned the paling stars, as each withdrew!

Yet I, even I, who am less than dust before you,
    Less than the lowest lintel of your door,
Was given one breathless midnight, to adore you.
    Fate, having granted this, can give no more!

Afridi Love

Since, oh, Beloved, you are not even faithful
  To me, who loved you so, for one short night,
For one brief space of darkness, though my absence
  Did but endure until the dawning light;

Since all your beauty—which was *mine*—you squandered
  On *that* which now lies dead across your door;
See here this knife, made keen and bright to kill you.
  You shall not see the sun rise any more.

Lie still! Lie still! In all the empty village
  Who is there left to hear or heed your cry?
All are gone to labour in the valley,
  Who will return before your time to die?

No use to struggle; when I found you sleeping,
  I took your hands and bound them to your side,
And both these slender feet, too apt at straying,
  Down to the cot on which you lie are tied.

Lie still, Beloved; that dead thing lying yonder,
  I hated and I killed, but love is sweet,
And you are more than sweet to me, who love you,
  Who decked my eyes with dust from off your feet.

Afridi Love

Give me your lips; ah, lovely and disloyal,
    Give me yourself again; before you go
Down through the darkness of the Great, Blind Portal,
    All of life's best and basest you must know.

Erstwhile, Beloved, you were so young and fragile
    I held you gently, as one holds a flower:
But now, God knows, what use to still be tender
    To one whose life is done within an hour?

I hurt? What then? Death will not hurt you, dearest,
    As you hurt me, for just a single night,
You call me cruel, who laid my life in ruins
    To gain one little moment of delight.

Look up, look out, across the open doorway
    The sunlight streams. The distant hills are blue.
Look at the pale, pink peach trees in our garden,
    Sweet fruit will come of them;—but not for you.

The fair, far snow, upon those jagged mountains
    That gnaw against the hard blue Afghan sky
Will soon descend, set free by summer sunshine.
    You will not see those torrents sweeping by.

The world is not for you. From this day forward,
    You must lie still alone; who would not lie
Alone for one night only, though returning
    I was, when earliest dawn should break the sky.

There lies my lute, and many strings are broken,
  Some one was playing it, and some one tore
The silken tassels round my Hookah woven;
  Some one who plays, and smokes, and loves, no more!

Some one who took last night his fill of pleasure,
  As I took mine at dawn! The knife went home
Straight through his heart! God only knows my rapture
  Bathing my chill hands in the warm red foam.

And so I pain you? This is only loving,
  Wait till I kill you! Ah, this soft, curled hair!
Surely the fault was mine, to love and leave you
  Even a single night, you are so fair.

Cold steel is very cooling to the fervour
  Of over-passionate ones, Beloved, like you.
Nay, turn your lips to mine. Not quite unlovely
  They are as yet, as yet, though quite untrue.

What will your brother say, to-night returning
  With laden camels homewards to the hills,
Finding you dead, and me asleep beside you,
  Will he awake me first before he kills?

For I shall sleep. Here on the cot beside you
  When you, my Heart's Delight, are cold in death.
When your young heart and restless lips are silent,
  Grown chilly, even beneath my burning breath.

When I have slowly drawn my knife across you,
    Taking my pleasure as I see you swoon,
I shall sleep sound, worn out by love's last fervour,
    And then, God grant your kinsmen kill me soon!

Yasmini

At night, when Passion's ebbing tide
    Left bare the Sands of Truth,
Yasmini, resting by my side,
    Spoke softly of her youth.

"And one," she said, "was tall and slim,
    Two crimson rose leaves made his mouth,
And I was fain to follow him
    Down to his village in the South.

"He was to build a hut hard by
    The stream where palms were growing,
We were to live, and love, and lie,
    And watch the water flowing.

"Ah, dear, delusive, distant shore,
    By dreams of futile fancy gilt!
The riverside we never saw,
    The palm leaf hut was never built!

"One had a Tope of Mangoe trees,
    Where early morning, noon and late,
The Persian wheels, with patient ease,
    Brought up their liquid, silver freight.

"And he was fain to rise and reach
    That garden sloping to the sea,
Whose groves along the wave-swept beach
    Should shelter him and love and me.

"Doubtless, upon that western shore
    With ripe fruit falling to the ground,
There dwells the Peace he hungered for,
    The lovely Peace we never found.

"Then there came one with eager eyes
    And keen sword, ready for the fray.
He missed the storms of Northern skies,
    The reckless raid and skirmish gay!

"He rose from dreams of war's alarms,
    To make his daggers keen and bright,
Desiring, in my very arms,
    The fiercer rapture of the fight!

"He left me soon; too soon, and sought
    The stronger, earlier love again.
News reached me from the Cabul Court,
    Afterwards nothing; doubtless slain.

"Doubtless his brilliant, haggard eyes,
    Long since took leave of life and light,
And those lithe limbs I used to prize
    Feasted the jackal and the kite.

"But the most loved! his sixteen years
   Shone in his cheeks' transparent red.
My kisses were his first: my tears
   Fell on his face when he was dead.

"He died, he died, I speak the truth,
   Though light love leave his memory dim,
He was the Lover of my Youth
   And all my youth went down with him.

"For passion ebbs and passion flows,
   But under every new caress
The riven heart more keenly knows
   Its own inviolate faithfulness.

"Our Gods are kind and still deem fit
   As in old days, with those to lie,
Whose silent hearths are yet unlit
   By the soft light of infancy.

"Therefore, one strange, mysterious night
   Alone within the Temple shade,
Recipient of a God's delight
   I lay enraptured, unafraid.

"Also to me the boon was given,
   But mourning quickly followed mirth,
My son, whose father stooped from Heaven,
   Died in the moment of his birth.

"When from the war beyond the seas
　　The reckless Lancers home returned,
Their spoils were laid across my knees,
　　About my lips their kisses burned.

"Back from the Comradeship of Death,
　　Free from the Friendship of the Sword,
With brilliant eyes and famished breath
　　They came to me for their reward.

"Why do I tell you all these things,
　　Baring my life to you, unsought?
When Passion folds his wearied wings
　　Sleep should be follower, never Thought.

"Ay, let us sleep. The window pane
　　Grows pale against the purple sky.
The dawn is with us once again,
　　The dawn; which always means good-bye."

Within her little trellised room, beside the palm-fringed sea,
She, wakeful in the scented gloom, spoke of her youth to me.

Ojira, to Her Lover

I AM waiting in the desert, looking out towards the sunset,
And counting every moment till we meet.
I am waiting by the marshes and I tremble and I listen
Till the soft sands thrill beneath your coming feet.

Till I see you, tall and slender, standing clear against the skyline,
A graceful shade across the lingering red,
While your hair the breezes ruffle, turns to silver in the twilight,
And makes a fair faint aureole round your head.

Far away towards the sunset I can see a narrow river,
That unwinds itself in red tranquillity;
I can hear its rippled meeting, and the gurgle of its greeting,
As it mingles with the loved and long sought sea.

In the purple sky above me showing dark against the starlight,
Long wavering flights of homeward birds fly low,
They cry each one to the other, and their weird and wistful calling,
Makes most melancholy music as they go.

Oh, my dearest, hasten, hasten! It is lonely here. Already
Have I heard the jackals' first assembling cry,
And among the purple shadows of the mangroves and the marshes
Fitful echoes of their footfalls passing by.

Ah, come soon! my arms are empty, and so weary for your beauty,
I am thirsty for the music of your voice.
Come to make the marshes joyous with the sweetness of your presence,
Let your nearing feet bid all the sands rejoice!

My hands, my lips are feverish with the longing and the waiting
And no softness of the twilight soothes their heat,
Till I see your radiant eyes, shining stars beneath the starlight,
Till I kiss the slender coolness of your feet.

Ah, loveliest, most reluctant, when you lay yourself beside me,
All the planets reel around me—fade away,
And the sands grow dim, uncertain,—I stretch out my hands towards you
While I try to speak but know not what I say!

I am faint with love and longing, and my burning eyes are gazing

Where the furtive Jackals wage their famished strife,
Oh, your shadow on the mangroves! and your step upon
                                            the sandhills,—
This is the loveliest evening of my Life!

Thoughts: Mahomed Akram

If some day this body of mine were burned
(It found no favour, alas! with you)
And the ashes scattered abroad, unurned,
Would Love die also, would Thought die too?
    But who can answer, or who can trust,
    No dreams would harry the windblown dust?

Were I laid away in the furrows deep,
Secure from jackal and passing plough,
Would your eyes not follow me still through sleep,
Torment me then as they torture now?
    Would you ever have loved me, Golden Eyes,
    Had I done aught better or otherwise?

Was I overspeechful, or did you yearn
When I sat silent, for songs or speech?
Ah, Beloved, I had been so apt to learn,
So apt, had you only cared to teach.
    But time for silence and song is done,
    You wanted nothing, my Golden Sun!

What should you want of a waning star?
That drifts in its lonely orbit far
Away from your soft, effulgent light
In outer planes of Eternal night?

Prayer

You are all that is lovely and light,
    Aziza whom I adore,
And, waking, after the night,
    I am weary with dreams of you.
Every nerve in my heart is tense and sore
    As I rise to another morning apart from you.

I dream of your luminous eyes,
    Aziza whom I adore!
Of the ruffled silk of your hair,
I dream, and the dreams are lies.
But I love them, knowing no more
    Will ever be mine of you
Aziza, my life's despair.

I would burn for a thousand days,
Aziza whom I adore,
Be tortured, slain, in unheard of ways
    If you pitied the pain I bore.
You pity! Your bright eyes, fastened on other things,
Are keener to sting my soul, than scorpion stings!

You are all that is lovely to me,
   All that is light,
One white rose in a Desert of weariness.
   I only live in the night,
The night, with its fair false dreams of you,
   You and your loveliness.

      Give me your love for a day,
        A night, an hour:
      If the wages of sin are Death
        I am willing to pay.
What is my life but a breath
   Of passion burning away?
Away for an unplucked flower.
   O Aziza whom I adore,
Aziza my one delight,
   Only one night, I will die before day,
And trouble your life no more.

The Aloe

My life was like an Aloe flower, beneath an orient sky,
Your sunshine touched it for an hour; it blossomed but to
die.

Torn up, cast out, on rubbish heaps where red flames work
their will
Each atom of the Aloe keeps the flower-time fragrance still.

Memory

How I loved you in your sleep,
With the starlight on your hair!

The touch of your lips was sweet,
   Aziza whom I adore,
I lay at your slender feet,
   And against their soft palms pressed,
I fitted my face to rest.
As winds blow over the sea
   From Citron gardens ashore,
Came, through your scented hair,
   The breeze of the night to me.

My lips grew arid and dry,
   My nerves were tense,
Though your beauty soothe the eye
   It maddens the sense.
Every curve of that beauty is known to me,
Every tint of that delicate roseleaf skin,
   And these are printed on every atom of me,
Burnt in on every fibre until I die.
   And for this, my sin,

I doubt if ever, though dust I be,
The dust will lose the desire,
The torment and hidden fire,
Of my passionate love for you.
   Aziza whom I adore,
My dust will be full of your beauty, as is the blue
And infinite ocean full of the azure sky.

In the light that waxed and waned
Playing about your slumber in silver bars,
As the palm trees swung their feathery fronds athwart the
                                                    stars,
How quiet and young you were,
Pale as the Champa flowers, violet veined,
That, sweet and fading, lay in your loosened hair.

How sweet you were in your sleep,
With the starlight on your hair!
Your throat thrown backwards, bare,
And touched with circling moonbeams, silver white
   On the couch's sombre shade.
O Aziza my one delight,
When Youth's passionate pulses fade,
And his golden heart beats slow,
When across the infinite sky
I see the roseate glow
Of my last, last sunset flare,
I shall send my thoughts to this night

And remember you as I die,
The one thing, among all the things of this earth, found fair.

How sweet you were in your sleep,
With the starlight, silver and sable, across your hair!

The First Lover

As o'er the vessel's side she leant,
  She saw the swimmer in the sea
With eager eyes on her intent,
  "Come down, come down and swim with me."

So weary was she of her lot,
  Tired of the ship's monotony,
She straightway all the world forgot
  Save the young swimmer in the sea.

So when the dusky, dying light
  Left all the water dark and dim,
She softly, in the friendly night,
  Slipped down the vessel's side to him.

Intent and brilliant, brightly dark,
  She saw his burning, eager eyes,
And many a phosphorescent spark
  About his shoulders fall and rise.

As through the hushed and Eastern night
  They swam together, hand in hand,

Or lay and laughed in sheer delight
   Full length upon the level sand.

"Ah, soft, delusive, purple night
   Whose darkness knew no vexing moon!
Ah, cruel, needless, dawning light
   That trembled in the sky too soon!"

Khan Zada's Song on the Hillside

The fires that burn on all the hills
   Light up the landscape grey,
The arid desert land distills
   The fervours of the day.

The clear white moon sails through the skies
   And silvers all the night,
I see the brilliance of your eyes
   And need no other light.

The death sighs of a thousand flowers
   The fervent day has slain
Are wafted through the twilight hours,
   And perfume all the plain.

My senses strain, and try to clasp
   Their sweetness in the air,
In vain, in vain; they only grasp
   The fragrance of your hair.

The plain is endless space expressed;
   Vast is the sky above,
I only feel, against your breast,
   Infinities of love.

Deserted Gipsy's Song: Hillside Camp

"She is glad to receive your turquoise ring,
    Dear and dark-eyed Lover of mine!
I, to have given you everything:
    Beauty maddens the soul like Wine.

"She is proud to have held aloof her charms,
    Slender, dark-eyed Lover of mine!
But I, of the night you lay in my arms:
    Beauty maddens the sense like Wine!

"She triumphs to think that your heart is won,
    Stately, dark-eyed Lover of mine!
I had not a thought of myself, not one:
    Beauty maddens the brain like Wine!

"She will speak you softly, while skies are blue,
    Dear, deluded Lover of mine!
I would lose both body and soul for you:
    Beauty maddens the brain like Wine!

"While the ways are fair she will love you well,
    Dear, disdainful Lover of mine!

But I would have followed you down to Hell:
    Beauty maddens the soul like Wine!

"Though you lay at her feet the days to be,
    Now no longer Lover of mine!
You can give her naught that you gave not me:
    Beauty maddened my soul like Wine!

"When the years have shown what is false or true:
    Beauty maddens the sight like Wine!
You will understand how I cared for you,
    First and only Lover of mine!"

The Plains

How one loves them,
These wide horizons; whether Desert or Sea,—
    Vague and vast and infinite; faintly clear—
Surely, hid in the far away, unknown "There,"
      Lie the things so longed for and found not, found
                      not, Here.

Only where some passionate, level land
    Stretches itself in reaches of golden sand,
Only where the sea line is joined to the sky-line, clear,
    Beyond the curve of ripple or white foamed
                            crest,—
      Shall the weary eyes
    Distressed by the broken skies,—
    Broken by Minaret, mountain, or towering
                            tree,—
Shall the weary eyes be assuaged,—be assuaged,—
                          and rest.

"Lost Delight"
After the Hazara War

I lie alone beneath the Almond blossoms,
    Where we two lay together in the spring,
And now, as then, the mountain snows are melting,
    This year, as last, the water-courses sing.

That was another spring, and other flowers,
    Hung, pink and fragile, on the leafless tree,
The land rejoiced in other running water,
    And I rejoiced, because you were with me.

You, with your soft eyes, darkly lashed and shaded,
    Your red lips like a living, laughing rose,
Your restless, amber limbs so lithe and slender
    Now lost to me. Gone whither no man knows.

You lay beside me singing in the sunshine;
    The rough, white fur, unloosened at the neck,
Showed the smooth skin, fair as the Almond blossoms,
    On which the sun could find no flaw or fleck.

I lie alone, beneath the Almond flowers,
  I hated them to touch you as they fell.
And now, who killed you? worse, ah, worse, who loves you?
  (My soul is burning as men burn in Hell.)

How I have sought you in the crowded cities!
  I have been mad, they say, for many days.
I know not how I came here, to the valley,
  What fate has led me, through what doubtful ways.

Somewhere I see my sword has done good service,
  Some one I killed, who, smiling, used your name,
But in what country? Nay, I have forgotten,
  All thought is shrivelled in my heart's hot flame.

Where are you now, Delight, and where your beauty,
  Your subtle curls, and laughing, changeful face?
Bound, bruised and naked (dear God, grant me patience),
  And sold in Cabul in the market-place.

I asked of you of all men. Who could tell me?
  Among so many captured, sold, or slain,
What fate was yours? (Ah, dear God, grant me patience,
  My heart is burnt, is burnt, with fire and pain.)

Oh, lost Delight! my heart is almost breaking,
  My sword is broken and my feet are sore,
The people look at me and say in passing,
  "He will not leave the village any more."

For as the evening falls, the fever rises,
    With frantic thoughts careering through the brain,
Wild thoughts of you. (Ah, dear God, grant me patience,
    My soul is hurt beyond all men call pain.)

I lie alone, beneath the Almond blossoms,
    And see the white snow melting on the hills
Till Khorassan is gay with water-courses,
    Glad with the tinkling sound of running rills,

And well I know that when the fragile petals
    Fall softly, ere the first green leaves appear,
(Ah, for these last few days, God, grant me patience,)
    Since Delight is not, I shall not be, here!

Unforgotten

Do you ever think of me? you who died
    Ere our Youth's first fervour chilled,
With your soft eyes and your pulses stilled
    Lying alone, aside,
Do you ever think of me, left in the light,
From the endless calm of your dawnless night?

I am faithful always: I do not say
    That the lips which thrilled to your lips of old
To lesser kisses are always cold;
    Had you wished for this in its narrow sense
    Our love perhaps had been less intense;
But as we held faithfulness, you and I,
    I am faithful always, as you who lie,
    Asleep for ever, beneath the grass,
    While the days and nights and the seasons pass,—
        Pass away.

I keep your memory near my heart,
    My brilliant, beautiful guiding Star,
Till long life over, I too depart
    To the infinite night where perhaps you are.

Oh, are you anywhere? Loved so well!
I would rather know you alive in Hell
Than think your beauty is nothing now,
With its deep dark eyes and tranquil brow
Where the hair fell softly. Can this be true
That nothing, nowhere, exists of you?
Nothing, nowhere, oh, loved so well
    I have *never* forgotten.
              Do you still keep
Thoughts of me through your dreamless sleep?

Oh, gone from me! lost in Eternal Night,
    Lost Star of light,
Risen splendidly, set so soon,
    Through the weariness of life's afternoon
        I dream of your memory yet.
My loved and lost, whom I could not save,
My youth went down with you to the grave,
Though other planets and stars may rise,
I dream of your soft and sorrowful eyes
    And I cannot forget.

Song of Faiz Ulla

Just at the time when Jasmins bloom, most sweetly in the summer weather,
Lost in the scented Jungle gloom, one sultry night we spent together,
We, Love and Night, together blent, a Trinity of tranced content.

Yet, while your lips were wholly mine, to kiss, to drink from, to caress,
We heard some far-off faint distress; harsh drop of poison in sweet wine
Lessening the fulness of delight,—
    Some quivering note of human pain,
Which rose and fell and rose again, in plaintive sobs throughout the night,

Spoiling the perfumed, moonless hours
We spent among the Jasmin flowers.

Story of Lilavanti

They lay the slender body down
  With all its wealth of wetted hair,
Only a daughter of the town,
  But very young and slight and fair.

The eyes, whose light one cannot see,
  Are sombre doubtless, like the tresses
The mouth's soft curvings seem to be
  A roseate series of caresses.

And where the skin has all but dried
  (The air is sultry in the room)
Upon her breast and either side,
  It shows a soft and amber bloom.

By women here, who knew her life,
  A leper husband, I am told,
Took all this loveliness to wife
  When it was barely ten years old.

And when the child in shocked dismay
  Fled from the hated husband's care

He caught and tied her, so they say,
  Down to his bedside by her hair.

To some low quarter of the town,
  Escaped a second time, she flew;
Her beauty brought her great renown
  And many lovers here she knew,

When, as the mystic Eastern night
  With purple shadow filled the air,
Behind her window framed in light,
  She sat with jasmin in her hair.

At last she loved a youth, who chose
  To keep this wild flower for his own,
He in his garden set his rose
  Where it might bloom for him alone.

Cholera came; her lover died,
  Want drove her to the streets again,
And women found her there, who tried
  To turn her beauty into gain.

But she who in those garden ways
  Had learnt of Love, would now no more
Be bartered in the market place
  For silver, as in days before.

That former life she strove to change;
    She sold the silver off her arms,
While all the world grew cold and strange
    To broken health and fading charms.

Till, finding lovers, but no friend,
    Nor any place to rest or hide,
She grew despairing at the end,
    Slipped softly down a well and died.

And yet, how short, when all is said,
    This little life of love and tears!
Her age, they say, beside her bed,
    To-day is only fifteen years.

The Garden by the Bridge

THE Desert sands are heated, parched and dreary,
  The tigers rend alive their quivering prey
In the near Jungle; here the kites rise, weary,
  Too gorged with living food to fly away.

All night the hungry jackals howl together
  Over the carrion in the river bed,
Or seize some small soft thing of fur or feather
  Whose dying shrieks on the night air are shed.

I hear from yonder Temple in the distance
  Whose roof with obscene carven Gods is piled,
Reiterated with a sad insistence
  Sobs of, perhaps, some immolated child.

Strange rites here, where the archway's shade is deeper,
  Are consummated in the river bed;
Pariahs steal the rotten railway sleeper
  To burn the bodies of their cholera dead.

But yet, their lust, their hunger, cannot shame them,
  Goaded by fierce desire, that flays and stings;

Poor beasts, and poorer men. Nay, who shall blame them?
   Blame the Inherent Cruelty of Things.

The world is horrible and I am lonely,
   Let me rest here where yellow roses bloom
And find forgetfulness, remembering only
   Your face beside me in the scented gloom.

Nay, do not shrink! I am not here for passion,
   I crave no love, only a little rest,
Although I would my face lay, lover's fashion,
   Against the tender coolness of your breast.

I am so weary of the Curse of Living
   The endless, aimless torture, tumult, fears.
Surely, if life were any God's free giving,
   He, seeing His gift, long since went blind with tears.

Seeing us; our fruitless strife, our futile praying,
   Our luckless Present and our bloodstained Past.
Poor players, who make a trick or two in playing,
   But know that death *must* win the game at last.

As round the Fowler, red with feathered slaughter,
   The little joyous lark, unconscious. sings,—
As the pink Lotus floats on azure water,
   Innocent of the mud from whence it springs.

You walk through life, unheeding all the sorrow,
    The fear and pain set close around your way,
Meeting with hopeful eyes each gay to-morrow,
    Living with joy each hour of glad to-day.

I love to have you thus (nay, dear, lie quiet,
    How should these reverent fingers wrong your hair?)
So calmly careless of the rush and riot
    That rages round, is seething everywhere.

You do not understand. You think your beauty
    Does but inflame my senses to desire,
Till all you hold as loyalty and duty,
    Is shrunk and shrivelled in the ardent fire.

You wrong me, wearied out with thought and grieving
    As though the whole world's sorrow eat my heart,
I come to gaze upon your face believing
    Its beauty is as ointment to the smart.

Lie still and let me in my desolation
    Caress the soft loose hair a moment's span.
Since Loveliness is Life's one Consolation,
    And love the only Lethe left to man.

Ah, give me here beneath the trees in flower,
    Beside the river where the fireflies pass,
One little dusky, all consoling hour
    Lost in the shadow of the long grown grass.

Give me, oh you whose arms are soft and slender,
  Whose eyes are nothing but one long caress,
Against your heart, so innocent and tender,
  A little Love and some Forgetfulness.

Fate Knows No Tears

Just as the dawn of Love was breaking
    Across the weary world of grey,
Just as my life once more was waking
    As roses waken late in May,
Fate, blindly cruel and havoc-making,
    Stepped in and carried you away.

Memories have I none in keeping
    Of times I held you near my heart,
Of dreams when we were near to weeping
    That dawn should bid us rise and part;
Never, alas, I saw you sleeping
    With soft closed eyes and lips apart,

Breathing my name still through your dreaming.—
    Ah! had you stayed, such things had been!
But Fate, unheeding human scheming,
    Serenely reckless came between—
Fate with her cold eyes hard and gleaming
    Unseared by all the sorrow seen.

Ah! well-beloved, I never told you,
    I did not show in speech or song,

How at the end I longed to fold you
    Close in my arms; so fierce and strong
The longing grew to have and hold you,
    You, and you only, all life long.

They who know nothing call me fickle,
    Keen to pursue and loth to keep.
Ah, could they see these tears that trickle
    From eyes erstwhile too proud to weep.
Could see me, prone, beneath the sickle,
    While pain and sorrow stand and reap!

Unopened scarce, yet overblown, lie
    The hopes that rose-like round me grew,
The lights are low, and more than lonely
    This life I lead apart from you.
Come back, come back! I want you only,
    And you who loved me never knew.

You loved me, pleaded for compassion
    On all the pain I would not share;
And I in weary, halting fashion
    Was loth to listen, long to care;
But now, dear God! I faint with passion
    For your far eyes and distant hair.

Yes, I am faint with love, and broken
    With sleepless nights and empty days;

I want your soft words fiercely spoken,
    Your tender looks and wayward ways—
Want that strange smile that gave me token
    Of many things that no man says.

Cold was I, weary, slow to waken
    Till, startled by your ardent eyes,
I felt the soul within me shaken
    And long-forgotten senses rise;
But in that moment you were taken,
    And thus we lost our Paradise!

Farewell, we may not now recover
    That golden "Then" misspent, passed by,
We shall not meet as loved and lover
    Here, or hereafter, you and I.
My time for loving you is over,
    Love has no future, but to die.

And thus we part, with no believing
    In any chance of future years.
We have no idle self-deceiving,
    No half-consoling hopes and fears;
We know the Gods grant no retrieving
    A wasted chance. Fate knows no tears.

Verses: Faiz Ulla

Just in the hush before dawn
A little wistful wind is born.
A little chilly errant breeze,
That thrills the grasses, stirs the trees.
And, as it wanders on its way,
While yet the night is cool and dark,
The first carol of the lark,—
Its plaintive murmurs seem to say
"I wait the sorrows of the day."

Two Songs by Sitara, of Kashmir

Beloved! your hair was golden
As tender tints of sunrise,
As corn beside the River
      In softly varying hues.
I loved you for your slightness,
Your melancholy sweetness,
Your changeful eyes, that promised
      What your lips would still refuse.

You came to me, and loved me,
Were mine upon the River,
The azure water saw us
      And the blue transparent sky;
The Lotus flowers knew it,
Our happiness together,
While life was only River,
      Only love, and you and I.

Love wakened on the River,
To sounds of running water,
With silver Stars for witness
      And reflected Stars for light;

Awakened to existence,
With ripples for first music
And sunlight on the River
    For earliest sense of sight.

Love grew upon the River
Among the scented flowers,
The open rosy flowers
    Of the Lotus buds in bloom—
Love, brilliant as the Morning,
More fervent than the Noon-day,
And tender as the Twilight
    In its blue transparent gloom.

Love died upon the River!
Cold snow upon the mountains,
The Lotus leaves turned yellow
    And the water very grey.
Our kisses faint and falter,
The clinging hands unfasten,
The golden time is over
    And our passion dies away.

    Away. To be forgotten,
    A ripple on the River,
    That flashes in the sunset,
    That flashed,—and died away.

Second Song: The Girl from Baltistan

                      Throb, throb, throb,
Far away in the blue transparent Night,
On the outer horizon of a dreaming consciousness,
She hears the sound of her lover's nearing boat
        Afar, afloat
On the river's loneliness, where the Stars are the only light;
    Hear the sound of the straining wood
        Like a broken sob
        Of a heart's distress,
    Loving misunderstood.

She lies, with her loose hair spent in soft disorder,
On a silken sheet with a purple woven border,
Every cell of her brain is latent fire,
Every fibre tense with restrained desire.
        And the straining oars sound clearer, clearer,
       The boat is approaching nearer, nearer;
      "How to wait through the moments' space
    Till I see the light of my lover's face?"

                    Throb, throb, throb,
The sound dies down the stream
Till it only clings at the senses' edge

Like a half-remembered dream.
    Doubtless, he in the silence lies,
      His fair face turned to the tender skies,
    Starlight touching his sleeping eyes.
While his boat caught in the thickset sedge
And the waters round it gurgle and sob,
    Or floats set free on the river's tide,
                           Oars laid aside.

She is awake and knows no rest,
Passion dies and is dispossessed
    Of his brief, despotic power.
But the Brain, once kindled, would still be afire
Were the whole world pasture to its desire,
And all of love, in a single hour,—
A single wine cup, filled to the brim,
                       Given to slake its thirst.

Some there are who are thus-wise cursed;
    Times that follow fulfilled desire
    Are of all their hours the worst.
They find no Respite and reach no Rest,
Though passion fail and desire grow dim,
    No assuagement comes from the thing possessed
        For possession feeds the fire.

  "Oh, for the life of the bright-hued things
    Whose marriage and death are one,

A floating fusion on golden wings,
　　Alit with passion and sun!

"But we who re-marry a thousand times,
　　As the spirit or senses will,
In a thousand ways, in a thousand climes,
　　We remain unsatisfied still."

As her lover left her, alone, awake she lies,
With a sleepless brain and weary, half-closed eyes.
She turns her face where the purple silk is spread,
Still sweet with delicate perfume his presence shed.
Her arms remembered his vanished beauty still,
And, reminiscent of clustered curls, her fingers thrill.
While the wonderful, Starlit Night wears slowly on
Till the light of another day, serene and wan,
　　　　　　　　　　Pierces the eastern skies.

Palm Trees by the Sea

*L*OVE, let me thank you for this!
   Now we have drifted apart,
Wandered away from the sea,—
   For the fresh touch of your kiss,
For the young warmth of your heart,
   For your youth given to me.

Thanks: for the curls of your hair,
   Softer than silk to the hand,
For the clear gaze of your eyes.
   For yourself: delicate, fair,
Seen as you lay on the sand,
   Under the violet skies.

Thanks: for the words that you said,—
   Secretly, tenderly sweet,
All through the tropical day,
   Till, when the sunset was red,
I, who lay still at your feet,
   Felt my life ebbing away,

Weary and worn with desire,
   Only yourself could console.

Love let me thank you for this!
   For that fierce fervour and fire
Burnt through my lips to my soul
   From the white heat of your kiss!

You were the essence of Spring,
   Wayward and bright as a flame:
Though we have drifted apart,
   Still how the syllables sing
Mixed in your musical name,
   Deep in the well of my heart!

Once in the lingering light,
   Thrown from the west on the Sea,
Laid you your garments aside,
   Slender and goldenly bright,
Glimmered your beauty, set free,
   Bright as a pearl in the tide.

Once, ere the thrill of the dawn
   Silvered the edge of the sea,
I, who lay watching you rest,—
   Pale in the chill of the morn
Found you still dreaming of me
   Stilled by love's fancies possessed.

Fallen on sorrowful days,
   Love, let me thank you for this,

You were so happy with me!
  Wrapped in Youth's roseate haze,
Wanting no more than my kiss
  By the blue edge of the sea!

Ah, for those nights on the sand
  Under the palms by the sea,
For the strange dream of those days
  Spent in the passionate land,
For your youth given to me,
  I am your debtor always!

Song by Gulbaz

"Is it safe to lie so lonely when the summer twilight closes,
No companion maidens, only you asleep among the roses?

"Thirteen, fourteen years you number, and your hair is soft and scented,
Perilous is such a slumber in the twilight all untented.

"Lonely loveliness means danger, lying in your rose-leaf nest,
What if some young passing stranger broke into your careless rest?"

But she would not heed the warning, lay alone serene and slight,
Till the rosy spears of morning slew the darkness of the night.

Young love, walking softly, found her, in the scented, shady closes,
Threw his ardent arms around her, kissed her lips beneath the roses.

And she said, with smiles and blushes, "Would that I had sooner known!
Never now the morning thrushes wake and find me all alone.

"Since you said the rose-leaf cover sweet protection gave, but slight,
I have found this dear young lover to protect me through the night!"

Kashmiri Song

Pale hands I loved beside the Shalimar,
    Where are you now? Who lies beneath your spell?
Whom do you lead on Rapture's roadway, far,
    Before you agonise them in farewell?

Oh, pale dispensers of my Joys and Pains,
    Holding the doors of Heaven and of Hell,
How the hot blood rushed wildly through the veins
    Beneath your touch, until you waved farewell.

Pale hands, pink tipped, like Lotus buds that float
    On those cool waters where we used to dwell,
I would have rather felt you round my throat,
    Crushing out life, than waving me farewell!

Reverie of Ormuz the Persian

Softly the feathery Palm-trees fade in the violet Distance,
Faintly the lingering light touches the edge of the sea,
Sadly the Music of Waves, drifts, faint as an Anthem's in-
sistence,
Heard in the aisles of a dream, over the sandhills, to me.

Now that the Lights are reversed, and the Singing changed
into sighing,
Now that the wings of our fierce, fugitive passion are
furled,
Take I unto myself, all alone in the light that is dying,
Much of the sorrow that lies hid at the Heart of the World.

Sad am I, sad for your loss: for failing the charm of your
presence,
Even the sunshine has paled, leaving the Zenith less blue.
Even the ocean lessens the light of its green opalescence,
Since, to my sorrow I loved, loved and grew weary of, you.

Why was our passion so fleeting, why had the flush of your
beauty
Only so slender a spell, only so futile a power?

Yet, even thus ever is life, save when long custom or duty
Moulds into sober fruit Love's fragile and fugitive flower.

Fain would my soul have been faithful; never an alien
                                    pleasure
Lured me away from the light lit in your luminous eyes,
But we have altered the World as pitiful man has leisure
To criticise, balance, take counsel, assuredly lies.

All through the centuries Man has gathered his flower, and
                                    fenced it,
—Infinite strife to attain; infinite struggle to keep,—
Holding his treasure awhile, all Fate and all forces against it,
Knowing it his no more, if ever his vigilance sleep.

But we have altered the World as pitiful man has grown
                                    stronger,
So that the things we love are as easily kept as won,
Therefore the ancient fight can engage and detain us no
                                    longer,
And all too swiftly, alas, passion is over and done.

Far too speedily now we can gather the coveted treasure,
Enjoy it awhile, be satiated, begin to tire;
And what shall be done henceforth with the profitless after-
                                    leisure,
Who has the breath to kindle the ash of a faded fire?

Ah, if it only had lasted! After my ardent endeavour
Came the delirious Joy, flooding my life like a sea,

Days of delight that are burnt on the brain for ever and ever,
Days and nights when you loved, before you grew weary of me.

Softly the sunset decreases dim in the violet Distance,
Even as Love's own fervour has faded away from me,
Leaving the weariness, the monotonous Weight of Existence,—
All the farewells in the world weep in the sound of the sea.

Sunstroke

Oh, straight, white road that runs to meet,
    Across green fields, the blue green sea,
You knew the little weary feet
    Of my child bride that was to be!

Her people brought her from the shore
    One golden day in sultry June,
And I stood, waiting, at the door,
    Praying my eyes might see her soon.

With eager arms, wide open thrown,
    Now never to be satisfied!
Ere I could make my love my own
    She closed her amber eyes and died.

Alas! alas! they took no heed
    How frail she was, my little one,
But brought her here with cruel speed
    Beneath the fierce, relentless sun.

We laid her on the marriage bed
    The bridal flowers in her hand,

A maiden from the ocean led
      Only, alas! to die inland.

I walk alone; the air is sweet,
      The white road wanders to the sea,
I dream of those two little feet
      That grew so tired in reaching me.

Adoration

WHO does not feel desire unending
    To solace through his daily strife,
With some mysterious Mental Blending,
    The hungry loneliness of life?

Until, by sudden passion shaken,
    As terriers shake a rat at play,
He finds, all blindly, he has taken
    The old, Hereditary way.

Yet, in the moment of communion,
    The very heart of passion's fire,
His spirit spurns the mortal union,
    "Not this, not this, the Soul's desire!"

    .   .   .   .   .

Oh You, by whom my life is riven,
    And reft away from my control,
Take back the hours of passion given!
    Love me one moment from your soul.

Although I once, in ardent fashion,
    Implored you long to give me this;

(In hopes to stem, or stifle, passion)
  Your hair to touch, your lips to kiss.

Now that your gracious self has granted
  The loveliness you hold as naught,
I find, alas! not that I wanted—
  Possession has not stifled Thought.

Desire its aim has only shifted,—
  Built hopes upon another plan,
And I in love for you have drifted
  Beyond all passion known to man.

Beyond all dreams of soft caresses
  The solacing of any kiss,—
Beyond the fragrance of your tresses
  (Once I had sold my soul for this!)

But now I crave no mortal union
  (Thanks for that sweetness in the past);
I need some subtle, strange communion,
  Some sense that *I* join *you* at last.

Long past the pulse and pain of passion,
  Long left the limits of all love,—
I crave some nearer, fuller fashion,
  Some unknown way, beyond, above,—

Some infinitely inner fusion,
    As Wave with Water; Flame with Fire,—
Let me dream once the dear delusion
    That I am You, oh, Heart's Desire!

Your kindness lent to my caresses
    That beauty you so lightly prize,—
The midnight of your sable tresses,
    The twilight of your shadowed eyes.

Ah, for that gift all thanks are given!
    Yet, oh, adored, beyond control,
Count all the passionate past forgiven
    And love me once, once, from your soul.

Three Songs of Zahir-u-Din

The tropic day's redundant charms
   Cool twilight soothes away,
The sun slips down behind the palms
   And leaves the landscape grey.
        I want to take you in my arms
        And kiss your lips away!

I wake with sunshine in my eyes
   And find the morning blue,
A night of dreams behind me lies
   And all were dreams of you!
        Ah, how I wish the while I rise,
        That what I dream were true.

The weary day's laborious pace,
   I hasten and beguile
By fancies, which I backwards trace
   To things I loved erstwhile;
        The weary sweetness of your face,
        Your faint, illusive smile.

The silken softness of your hair
   Where faint bronze shadows are,

Your strangely slight and youthful air,
  No passions seem to mar,—
      Oh, why, since Fate has made you fair,
      Must Fortune keep you far?

Thus spent, the day so long and bright
  Less hot and brilliant seems,
Till in a final flare of light
  The sun withdraws his beams.
      Then, in the coolness of the night,
      I meet you in my dreams!

Second Song

How much I loved that way you had
Of smiling most, when very sad,
A smile which carried tender hints
    Of delicate tints
    And warbling birds,
    Of sun and spring,
And yet, more than all other thing,
Of Weariness beyond all Words!

None other ever smiled that way,
    None that I know,—
The essence of all Gaiety lay,
Of all mad mirth that men may know,
In that sad smile, serene and slow,
That on your lips was wont to play.

It needed many delicate lines
And subtle curves and roseate tints
To make that weary radiant smile;
It flickered, as beneath the vines
The sunshine through green shadow glints
On the pale path that lies below,

Flickered and flashed, and died away,
But the strange thoughts it woke meanwhile
    Were wont to stay.

Thoughts of Strange Things you used to know
In dim, dead lives, lived long ago,
Some madly mirthful Merriment
Whose lingering light is yet unspent,—
Some unimaginable Woe,—
Your strange, sad smile forgets these not,
Though you, yourself, long since, forgot!

Third Song, Written During Fever

To-night the clouds hang very low,
    They take the Hill-tops to their breast,
    And lay their arms about the fields.
The wind that fans me lying low,
    Restless with great desire for rest,
    No cooling touch of freshness yields.

I, sleepless through the stifling heat,
    Watch the pale Lightning's constant glow
    Between the wide set open doors.
I lie and long amidst the heat,—
    The fever that my senses know,
    For that cool slenderness of yours.

So delicate and cool you are!
    A roseleaf that has lain in snow,
    A snowflake tinged with sunset fire.
You do not know, so young you are,
    How Fever fans the senses' glow
    To uncontrollable desire!

And fills the spaces of the night
    With furious and frantic thought,

One would not dare to think by day.
Ah, if you came to me to-night
These visions would be turned to naught,
These hateful dreams be held at bay!

But you are far, and Loneliness
My only lover through the night;
And not for any word or prayer
Would you console my loneliness
Or lend yourself, serene and slight,
And the cool clusters of your hair.

All through the night I long for you,
As shipwrecked men in tropics yearn
For the fresh flow of streams and springs.
My fevered fancies follow you
As dying men in deserts turn
Their thoughts to clear and chilly things.

Such dreams are mine, and such my thirst,
Unceasing and unsatisfied,
Until the night is burnt away
Among these dreams and fevered thirst,
And, through the open doorways, glide
The white feet of the coming day.

The Regret of the Ranee in the Hall of Peacocks

This man has taken my husband's life
   And laid my Brethren low,
No sister indeed, were I, no wife,
   To pardon and let him go.

Yet why does he look so young and slim
   As he weak and wounded lies?
How hard for me to be harsh to him
   With his soft, appealing eyes.

His hair is ruffled upon the stone
   And the slender wrists are bound,
So young! and yet he has overthrown
   His scores on the battle ground.

Would I were only a slave to-day,
   To whom it were right and meet
To wash the stains of the War away,
   The dust from the weary feet.

Were I but one of my serving girls
  To solace his pain to rest!
Shake out the sand from the soft loose curls,
  And hold him against my breast!

Have we such beauty around our Throne?
  Such lithe and delicate strength?
Would God that I were the senseless stone
  To support his slender length!

I hate those wounds that trouble my sight,
  Unknown! how I wish you lay,
Alone in my silken tent to-night
  While I charmed the pain away.

I would lay you down on the Royal bed,
  I would bathe your wounds with wine,
And setting your feet against my head
  Dream you were lover of mine.

My Crown is heavy upon my hair,
  The jewels weigh on my breast,
All I would leave, with delight, to share
  Your pale and passionate rest!

But hands grow restless about their swords,
  Lips murmur below their breath,
"The Queen is silent too long!" "My Lords.
  —Take him away to death!"

Protest: By Zahir-u-Din

Alas! alas! this wasted Night
With all its Jasmin-scented air,
Its thousand stars, serenely bright!
I lie alone, and long for you,
Long for your Champa-scented hair,
Your tranquil eyes of twilight hue;

Long for the close-curved, delicate lips
—Their sinuous sweetness laid on mine—
Here, where the slender fountain drips,
Here, where the yellow roses glow,
Pale in the tender silver shine
The stars across the garden throw.

Alas! alas! poor passionate Youth!
Why must we spend these lonely **nights?**
The poets hardly speak the truth,—
Despite their praiseful litany,
His season is not all delights
Nor every night an ecstasy!

The very power and passion that **make**—
Might make—his days one golden **dream,**

How he must suffer for their sake!
Till, in their fierce and futile rage,
The baffled senses almost deem
They might be happier in old age.

Age that can find red roses sweet,
And yet not crave a rose-red mouth;
Hear Bulbuls, with no wish that feet
Of sweeter singers went his way;
Inhale warm breezes from the South,
Yet never feel his fancy stray.

From some near Village I can hear
The cadenced throbbing of a drum,
Now softly distant, now more near;
And in an almost human fashion,
It, plaintive, wistful, seems to come
Laden with sighs of fitful passion,

To mock me, lying here alone
Among the thousand useless flowers
Upon the fountain's border-stone—
Cold stone, that chills me as I lie
Counting the slowly passing hours
By the white spangles in the sky.

Some feast the Tom-toms celebrate,
Where, close together, side by side,

Gay in their gauze and tinsel state
With lips serene and downcast eyes,
Sit the young bridegroom and his bride,
While round them songs and laughter rise.

They are together; why are we
So hopelessly, so far apart?
Oh, I implore you, come to me!
Come to me, Solace of mine eyes!
Come, Consolation of my heart!
Light of my senses! What replies?

A little, languid, mocking breeze
That rustles through the Jasmin flowers
And stirs among the Tamarind trees;
A little gurgle of the spray
That drips, unheard, through silent hours,
Then breaks in sudden bubbling play.

Wind, have you never loved a rose?
And water, seek you not the Sea?
Why, therefore, mock at my repose?
Is it my fault I am alone
Beneath the feathery Tamarind tree
Whose shadows over me are thrown?

Nay, I am mad indeed, with thirst
For all to me this night denied

And drunk with longing, and accurst
Beyond all chance of sleep or rest,
With love, unslaked, unsatisfied,
And dreams of beauty unpossessed.

Hating the hour that brings you not,
Mad at the space betwixt us twain,
Sad for my empty arms, so hot
And fevered, even the chilly stone
Can scarcely cool their burning pain,—
And oh, this sense of being alone!

Take hence, O Night, your wasted hours,
You bring me not my Life's Delight,
My Star of Stars, my Flower of Flowers!
You leave me loveless and forlorn,
Pass on, most false and futile night,
Pass on, and perish in the Dawn!

Famine Song

Death and Famine on every side
    And never a sign of rain,
The bones of those who have starved and died
    Unburied upon the plain.
What care have I that the bones bleach white?
    To-morrow they may be mine,
But I shall sleep in your arms to-night
    And drink your lips like wine!

Cholera, Riot, and Sudden Death,
    And the brave red blood set free,
The glazing eye and the failing breath,—
    But what are these things to me?
Your breath is quick and your eyes are bright
    And your blood is red like wine,
And I shall sleep in your arms to-night
    And hold your lips with mine!

I hear the sound of a thousand tears,
    Like softly pattering rain,
I see the fever, folly, and fears
    Fulfilling man's tale of pain.

But for the moment your star is bright,
    I revel beneath its shine,
For I shall sleep in your arms to-night
    And feel your lips on mine!

And you need not deem me over cold,
    That I do not stop to think
For all the pleasure this Life may hold
    Is on the Precipice brink.
Thought could but lessen my soul's delight,
    And to-day she may not pine.
For I shall lie in your arms to-night
    And close your lips with mine!

I trust what sorrow the Fates may send
    I may carry quietly through,
And pray for grace when I reach the end,
    To die as a man should do.
To-day, at least, must be clear and bright,
    Without a sorrowful sign,
Because I sleep in your arms to-night
    And feel your lips on mine!

So on I work, in the blazing sun,
    To bury what dead we may,
But glad, oh, glad, when the day is done
    And the night falls round us grey.

Would those we covered away from sight
    Had a rest as sweet as mine!
For I shall sleep in your arms to-night
    And drink your lips like wine!

The Window Overlooking the Harbour

Sad is the Evening: all the level sand
  Lies left and lonely, while the restless sea,
Tired of the green caresses of the land,
  Withdraws into its own infinity.

But still more sad this white and chilly Dawn
  Filling the vacant spaces of the sky,
While little winds blow here and there forlorn
  And all the stars, weary of shining, die.

And more than desolate, to wake, to rise,
  Leaving the couch, where softly sleeping still,
What through the past night made my heaven, lies;
  And looking out across the window sill

See, from the upper window's vantage ground,
  Mankind slip into harness once again,
And wearily resume his daily round
  Of love and labour, toil and strife and pain.

How the sad thoughts slip back across the night:
  The whole thing seems so aimless and so vain.

What use the raptures, passion and delight,
    Burnt out; as though they could not wake again.

The worn-out nerves and weary brain repeat
    The question: whither all these passions tend;—
This curious thirst, so painful and so sweet,
    So fierce, so very short-lived, to what end?

Even, if seeking for ourselves, the Race,
    The only immortality we know,—
Even if from the flower of our embrace
    Some spark should kindle, or some fruit should grow,

What were the use? the gain, to us or it,
    That we should cause another You or Me,—
Another life, from our light passion lit,
    To suffer like ourselves awhile and die.

What aim, what end indeed? Our being runs
    In a closed circle. All we know or see
Tends to assure us that a thousand Suns,
    Teeming perchance with life, have ceased to be.

Ah, the grey Dawn seems more than desolate,
    And the past night of passion worse than waste,
Love but a useless flower, that soon or late,
    Turns to a fruit with bitter aftertaste.

Youth, even Youth, seems futile and forlorn
    While the new day grows slowly white above.
Pale and reproachful comes the chilly Dawn
    After the fervour of a night of love.

Back to the Border

The tremulous morning is breaking
    Against the white waste of the sky,
And hundreds of birds are awaking
    In tamarisk bushes hard by.
I, waiting alone in the station,
    Can hear in the distance, grey-blue,
The sound of that iron desolation,
    The train that will bear me from you.

'T will carry me under your casement,
    You'll feel in your dreams as you lie
The quiver, from gable to basement,
    The rush of my train sweeping by.
And I shall look out as I pass it,—
    Your dear, unforgettable door,
'T was *ours* till last night, but alas! it
    Will never be mine any more.

Through twilight blue-grey and uncertain,
    Where frost leaves the window-pane free,
I'll look at the tinsel-edged curtain
    That hid so much pleasure for me.

I go to my long undone duty
  Alone in the chill and the gloom,
My eyes are still full of the beauty
  I leave in your rose-scented room.

Lie still in your dreams; for your tresses
  Are free of my lingering kiss.
I keep you awake with caresses
  No longer; be happy in this!
From passion you told me you hated
  You're now and for ever set free,
I pass in my train, sorrow-weighted,
  Your house that was Heaven to me.

You won't find a trace, when you waken,
  Of me or my love of the past,
Rise up and rejoice! I have taken
  My longed-for departure at last.
My fervent and useless persistence
  You never need suffer again,
Nor even perceive in the distance
  The smoke of my vanishing train!

Reverie: Zahir-u-Din

ALONE, I wait, till her twilight gate
                The Night slips quietly through,
With shadow and gloom, and purple bloom,
                Flung over the Zenith blue.

Her stars that tremble, would fain dissemble
                Light over lovers thrown,—
Her hush and mystery know no history
                Such as day may own.
Day has record of pleasure and pain,
But things that are done by Night remain
                For ever and ever unknown.

For a thousand years, 'neath a thousand skies,
                Night has brought men love;
Therefore the old, old longings rise
                As the light grows dim above.

Therefore, now that the shadows close,
                And the mists weird and white,
While Time is scented with musk and rose;
                Magic with silver light.

I long for love; will you grant me some?
    Day is over at last.
Come! as lovers have always come,
    Through the evenings of the Past.
Swiftly, as lovers have always come,
Softly, as lovers have always come
    Through the long-forgotten Past.

Sea Song

Against the planks of the cabin side,
    (So slight a thing between them and me,)
The great waves thundered and throbbed and sighed,
    The great green waves of the Indian sea!

Your face was white as the foam is white,
    Your hair was curled as the waves are curled,
I would we had steamed and reached that night
    The sea's last edge, the end of the world.

The wind blew in through the open port,
    So freshly joyous and salt and free,
Your hair it lifted, your lips it sought,
    And then swept back to the open sea.

The engines throbbed with their constant beat;
    Your heart was nearer, and all I heard;
Your lips were salt, but I found them sweet,
    While, acquiescent, you spoke no word.

So straight you lay in your narrow berth,
    Rocked by the waves; and you seemed to be

Essence of all that is sweet on earth,
    Of all that is sad and strange at sea.

And you were white as the foam is white,
    Your hair was curled as the waves are curled.
Ah! had we but sailed and reached that night,
    The sea's last edge, the end of the world!

To the Hills!

'Tis eight miles out and eight miles in,
    Just at the break of morn.
'T is ice without and flame within,
    To gain a kiss at dawn!

Far, where the Lilac Hills arise
    Soft from the misty plain,
A lone enchanted hollow lies
    Where I at last drew rein.

Midwinter grips this lonely land,
    This stony, treeless waste,
Where East, due East, across the sand,
    We fly in fevered haste.

Pull up! the East will soon be red,
    The wild duck westward fly,
And make above my anxious head,
    Triangles in the sky.

Like wind we go; we both are still
    So young; all thanks to Fate!

(It cuts like knives, this air so chill,)
    Dear God! if I am late!

Behind us, wrapped in mist and sleep
    The Ruined City lies,
(Although we race, we seem to creep!)
    While lighter grow the skies.

Eight miles out only, eight miles in,
    Good going all the way;
But more and more the clouds begin
    To redden into day.

And every snow-tipped peak grows pink,
    An iridescent gem!
My heart beats quick, with joy, to think
    How I am nearing them!

As mile on mile behind us falls,
    Till, oh, delight! I see
My Heart's Desire, who softly calls
    Across the gloom to me.

The utter joy of that First Love
    No later love has given,
When, while the skies grew light above,
    We entered into Heaven.

Till I Wake

When I am dying, lean over me tenderly, softly,
  Stoop, as the yellow roses droop in the wind from the South.
So I may, when I wake, if there be an Awakening,
  Keep, what lulled me to sleep, the touch of your lips on my mouth.

His Rubies: Told by Valgovind

Along the hot and endless road,
  Calm and erect, with haggard eyes,
The prisoner bore his fetters' load
  Beneath the scorching, azure skies.

Serene and tall, with brows unbent,
  Without a hope, without a friend,
He, under escort, onward went,
  With death to meet him at the end.

The Poppy fields were pink and gay
  On either side, and in the heat
Their drowsy scent exhaled all day
  A dream-like fragrance almost sweet.

And when the cool of evening fell
  And tender colours touched the sky,
He still felt youth within him dwell
  And half forgot he had to die.

Sometimes at night, the Camp-fires lit
  And casting fitful light around,

His guard would, friend-like, let him sit
    And talk awhile with them, unbound.

Thus they, the night before the last,
    Were resting, when a group of girls
Across the small encampment passed,
    With laughing lips and scented curls.

Then in the Prisoner's weary eyes
    A sudden light lit up once more,
The women saw him with surprise,
    And pity for the chains he bore.

For little women reck of Crime
    If young and fair the criminal be
Here in this tropic, amorous clime
    Where love is still untamed and free.

And one there was, she walked less fast,
    Behind the rest, perhaps beguiled
By his lithe form, who, as she passed,
    Waited a little while, and smiled.

The guard, in kindly Eastern fashion,
    Smiled to themselves, and let her stay.
So tolerant of human passion,
    "To love he has but one more day."

Yet when (the soft and scented gloom
    Scarce lighted by the dying fire)
His arms caressed her youth and bloom,
    With him it was not all desire.

"For me," he whispered, as he lay,
    "But little life remains to live.
One thing I crave to take away:
    You have the gift; but will you give?

"If I could know some child of mine
    Would live his life, and see the sun
Across these fields of poppies shine,
    What should I care that mine is done?

"To die would not be dying quite,
    Leaving a little life behind,
You, were you kind to me to-night,
    Could grant me this; but—are you kind?

"See, I have something here for you
    For you and It, if It there be."
Soft in the gloom her glances grew,
    With gentle tears he could not see.

He took the chain from off his neck,
    Hid in the silver chain there lay

Three rubies, without flaw or fleck.
　　She answered softly, "I will stay."

He drew her close; the moonless skies
　　Shed little light; the fire was dead.
Soft pity filled her youthful eyes,
　　And many tender things she said.

Throughout the hot and silent night
　　All that he asked of her she gave.
And, left alone ere morning light,
　　He went serenely to the grave,

Happy; for even when the rope
　　Confined his neck, his thoughts were free,
And centered round his Secret Hope,
　　The little life that was to be.

When Poppies bloomed again, she bore
　　His child who gaily laughed and crowed,
While round his tiny neck he wore
　　The rubies given on the road.

For his small sake she wished to wait,
　　But vainly to forget she tried,
And grieving for the Prisoner's fate,
　　She broke her gentle heart and died.

Song of Taj Mahomed

Dear is my inlaid sword; across the Border
It brought me much reward; dear is my Mistress,
The jewelled treasure of an amorous hour.
Dear beyond measure are my dreams and Fancies.

These I adore; for these I live and labour,
Holding them more than sword or jewelled Mistress,
For this indeed may rust, and that prove faithless,
But, till my limbs are dust, I have my Fancies.

The Garden of Kama: Kama the Indian Eros

The daylight is dying,
The Flying fox flying,
    Amber and amethyst burn in the sky.
See, the sun throws a late,
Lingering, roseate
    Kiss to the landscape to bid it good-bye.

The time of our Trysting!
Oh, come, unresisting,
    Lovely, expectant, on tentative feet.
Shadow shall cover us,
Roses bend over us,
    Making a bride chamber, sacred and sweet.

We know not life's reason,
The length of its season,
    Know not if they know, the great Ones above.
We none of us sought it,
And few could support it,
    Were it not gilt with the glamour of love.

But much is forgiven
To Gods who have given,
    If but for an hour, the Rapture of Youth.
You do not yet know it,
But Kama shall show it,
    Changing your dreams to his Exquisite Truth.

The Fireflies shall light you,
And naught shall affright you,
    Nothing shall trouble the Flight of the Hours.
Come, for I wait for you,
Night is too late for you,
    Come, while the twilight is closing the flowers.

Every breeze still is,
And, scented with lilies,
    Cooled by the twilight, refreshed by the dew,
The garden lies breathless,
Where Kama, the Deathless,
    In the hushed starlight, is waiting for you.

Camp Follower's Song, Gomal River

We have left Gul Kach behind us,
    Are marching on Apozai,—
Where pleasure and rest are waiting
    To welcome us by and by.

We're falling back from the Gomal,
    Across the Gir-dao plain,
The camping ground is deserted,
    We'll never come back again.

Along the rocks and the defiles,
    The mules and the camels wind.
Good-bye to Rahimut-Ullah,
    The man who is left behind.

For some we lost in the skirmish,
    And some were killed in the fight,
But he was captured by fever,
    In the sentry pit, at night.

A rifle shot had been swifter,
    Less trouble a sabre thrust,
But his Fate decided fever,
    And each man dies as he must.

Behind us, red in the distance,
    The wavering flames rise high,
The flames of our burning grass-huts,
    Against the black of the sky.

We hear the sound of the river,
    An ever-lessening moan,
The hearts of us all turn backwards
    To where he is left alone.

We sing up a little louder,
    We know that we feel bereft,
We're leaving the camp together,
    And only one of us left.

The only one, out of many,
    And each must come to his end,
I wish I could stop this singing,
    He happened to be my friend.

We're falling back from the Gomal
    We're marching on Apozai,

And pleasure and rest are waiting
 To welcome us by and by.

Perhaps the feast will taste bitter,
 The lips of the girls less kind,—
Because of Rahimut-Ullah,
 The man who is left behind!

Song of the Colours:
by Taj Mahomed

Rose-colour

Rose Pink am I, the colour gleams and glows
   In many a flower; her lips, those tender doors
By which, in time of love, love's essence flows
   From him to her, are dyed in delicate Rose.
Mine is the earliest Ruby light that pours
   Out of the East, when day's white gates unclose.

On downy peach, and maiden's downier cheek
   I, in a flush of radiant bloom, alight,
Clinging, at sunset, to the shimmering peak
   I veil its snow in floods of Roseate light.

Azure

Mine is the heavenly hue of Azure skies,
   Where the white clouds lie soft as seraphs' wings,
Mine the sweet, shadowed light in innocent eyes,
   Whose lovely looks light only on lovely things.

Mine the Blue Distance, delicate and clear,
   Mine the Blue Glory of the morning sea,

All that the soul so longs for, finds not here,
  Fond eyes deceive themselves, and find in me.

Scarlet
HAIL! to the Royal Red of living Blood,
  Let loose by steel in spirit-freeing flood,
Forced from faint forms, by toil or torture torn
  Staining the patient gates of life new born.

Colour of War and Rage, of Pomp and Show,
  Banners that flash, red flags that flaunt and glow,
Colour of Carnage, Glory, also Shame,
  Raiment of women women may not name.

I hide in mines, where unborn Rubies dwell,
  Flicker and flare in fitful fire in Hell,
The outpressed life-blood of the grape is mine,
  Hail! to the Royal Purple Red of Wine.

Strong am I, over strong, to eyes that tire,
  In the hot hue of Rapine, Riot, Flame.
Death and Despair are black, War and Desire,
  The two red cards in Life's unequal game.

Green
I AM the Life of Forests, and Wandering Streams,
  Green as the feathery reeds the Florican love,
Young as a maiden, who of her marriage dreams,
  Still sweetly inexperienced in ways of Love.

Colour of Youth and Hope, some waves are mine,
  Some emerald reaches of the evening sky.
See, in the Spring, my sweet green Promise shine,
  Never to be fulfilled, of by and by.

Never to be fulfilled; leaves bud, and ever
  Something is wanting, something falls behind;
The flowered Solstice comes indeed, but never
  That light and lovely summer men divined.

Violet
I WERE the colour of Things, (if hue they had)
    That are hard to name.
Of curious, twisted thoughts that men call "mad"
    Or oftener "shame."
Of that delicate vice, that is hardly vice,
    So reticent, rare,
Ethereal, as the scent of buds and spice,
    In this Eastern air.

On palm-fringed shores I colour the Cowrie shell,
    With its edges curled;
And, deep in Datura poison buds, I dwell
    In a perfumed world.
My lilac tinges the edge of the evening sky
    Where the sunset clings.
My purple lends an Imperial Majesty
    To the robes of kings.

Yellow
Gold am I, and for me, ever men curse and pray,
  Selling their souls and each other, by night and day.
A sordid colour, and yet, I make some things fair,
  Dying sunsets, fields of corn, and a maiden's hair.

Thus they discoursed in the daytime,—Violet, Yellow, and Blue,
  Emerald, Scarlet, and Rose-colour, the pink and perfect hue.
Thus they spoke in the sunshine, when their beauty was manifest,
  Till the Night came, and the Silence, and gave them an equal rest.

Lalila, to the Ferengi Lover

Why above others was I so blessed
    And honoured? to be chosen one
To hold you, sleeping, against my breast,
    As now I may hold your only son.

Twelve months ago; that wonderful night!
    You gave your life to me in a kiss;
Have I done well, for that past delight,
    In return, to have given you this?

Look down at his face, your face, beloved,
    His eyes are azure as yours are blue.
In every line of his form is proved
    How well I loved you, and only you.

I felt the secret hope at my heart
    Turned suddenly to the living joy,
And knew that your life and mine had part
    As golden grains in a brass alloy.

And learning thus, that your child was mine,
    Thrilled by the sense of its stirring life,

I held myself as a sacred shrine
    Afar from pleasure, and pain, and strife,

That all unworthy I might not be
    Of that you had deigned to cause to dwell
Hidden away in the heart of me,
    As white pearls hide in a dusky shell.

Do you remember, when first you laid
    Your lips on mine, that enchanted night?
My eyes were timid, my lips afraid,
    You seemed so slender and strangely white.

I always tremble; the moments flew
    Swiftly to dawn that took you away,
But this is a small and lovely you
    Content to rest in my arms all day.

Oh, since you have sought me, Lord, for this,
    And given your only child to me,
My life devoted to yours and his,
    Whilst I am living, will always be.

And after death, through the long To Be,
    (Which, I think, must surely keep love's laws,)
I, should you chance to have need of me,
    Am ever and always, only yours.

On the City Wall

Upon the City Ramparts, lit up by sunset gleam,
The Blue eyes that conquer, meet the Darker eyes that dream.

The Dark eyes, so Eastern, and the Blue eyes from the West,
The last alight with action, the first so full of rest.

Brown, that seem to hold the Past; its magic mystery,
Blue, that catch the early light, of ages yet to be.

Meet and fall and meet again, then linger, look, and smile,
Time and distance all forgotten, for a little while.

Happy on the city wall, in the warm spring weather,
All the force of Nature's laws, drawing them together.

East and West so gaily blending, for a little space,
All the sunshine seems to centre, round th' Enchanted place!

One rides down the dusty road, one watches from the wall,
Azure eyes would fain return, and Amber eyes recall;

Would fain be on the ramparts, and resting heart to heart,
But time o' love is overpast, East and West must part.

Blue eyes so clear and brilliant! Brown eyes so dark and deep!
Those are dim, and ride away, these cry themselves to sleep.

*"Oh, since Love is all so short, the sob so near the smile,
Blue eyes that always conquer us, is it worth your while?"*

"Love Lightly"

There were Roses in the hedges, and Sunshine in the sky,
Red Lilies in the sedges, where the water rippled by,
A thousand Bulbuls singing, oh, how jubilant they were,
And a thousand flowers flinging their sweetness on the air.

But you, who sat beside me, had a shadow in your eyes,
Their sadness seemed to chide me, when I gave you scant re-
plies;
You asked "Did I remember?" and "When had I ceased to
care?"
In vain you fanned the ember, for the love flame was not
there.

"And so, since you are tired of me, you ask me to forget,
  What is the use of caring, now that you no longer care?
When Love is dead his Memory can only bring regret,
  But how can I forget you with the flowers in your hair?"

What use the scented Roses, or the azure of the sky?
They are sweet when Love reposes, but then he had to die.
What could I do in leaving you, but ask you to forget,—
I suffered, too, in grieving you; I all but loved you yet.

But half love is a treason, that no lover can forgive,
I had loved you for a season, I had no more to give.
You saw my passion faltered, for I could but let you see,
And it was not I that altered, but Fate that altered me.

And so, since I am tired of love, I ask you to forget,
    What is the use you caring, now that I no longer care?
When Love is dead, his Memory can only bring regret;
    Forget me, oh, forget me, and my flower-scented hair!

No Rival Like the Past

As those who eat a Luscious Fruit, sunbaked,
    Full of sweet juice, with zest, until they find
It finished, and their appetite unslaked,
    And so return and eat the pared-off rind;—

We, who in Youth, set white and careless teeth
    In the Ripe Fruits of Pleasure while they last,
Later, creep back to gnaw the cast-off sheath,
    And find there is no Rival like the Past.

Verse by Taj Mahomed

When first I loved, I gave my very soul
Utterly unreserved to Love's control,
But Love deceived me, wrenched my youth away
And made the gold of life for ever grey.
Long I lived lonely, yet I tried in vain
With any other Joy to stifle pain;
There *is* no other joy, I learned to know,
And so returned to Love, as long ago.
Yet I, this little while ere I go hence,
Love very lightly now, in self-defence.

Lines by Taj Mahomed

This passion is but an ember
    Of a Sun, of a Fire, long set;
I could not live and remember,
    And so I love and forget.

You say, and the tone is fretful,
    That my mourning days were few,
You call me over-forgetful—
    My God, if you only knew!

There Is No Breeze to Cool the Heat of Love

The listless Palm-trees catch the breeze above
   The pile-built huts that edge the salt Lagoon,
There is no Breeze to cool the heat of love,
   No wind from land or sea, at night or noon.

Perfumed and robed I wait, my Lord, for you,
   And my heart waits alert, with strained delight,
My flowers are loath to close, as though they knew
   That you will come to me before the night.

In the Verandah all the lights are lit,
   And softly veiled in rose to please your eyes,
Between the pillars flying foxes flit,
   Their wings transparent on the lilac skies.

Come soon, my Lord, come soon, I almost fear
   My heart may fail me in this keen suspense,
Break with delight, at last, to know you near.
   Pleasure is one with Pain, if too intense.

I envy these: the steps that you will tread,
    The jasmin that will touch you by its leaves,
When, in your slender height, you stoop your head
    At the low door beneath the palm-thatched eaves.

For though you utterly belong to me,
    And love has done his utmost 'twixt us twain,
Your slightest, careless touch yet seems to be
    That keen delight so much akin to pain.

The night breeze blows across the still Lagoon,
    And stirs the Palm-trees till they wave above
Our pile-built huts; oh, come, my Lord, come soon,
    There is no Breeze to cool the heat of love.

Every time you give yourself to me,
    The gift seems greater, and yourself more fair,
This slight-built, palm-thatched hut has come to be
    A temple, since, my Lord, you visit there.

And as the water, gurgling softly, goes
    Among the piles beneath the slender floor,
I hear it murmur, as it seaward flows,
    Of the great Wonder seen upon the shore.

The Miracle, that you should come to me,
    Whom the whole world, seeing, can but desire,
It is as though some White Star stooped to be
    The messmate of our little cooking fire.

Leaving the Glory of his Purple Skies,
    And the White Friendship of the Crescent Moon,
And yet;—I look into your brilliant eyes,
    And find content; oh, come, my Lord, some soon.

Perfumed and robed I wait for you, I wait,
    The flowers that please you wreathed about my hair,
And this poor face set forth in jewelled state,
    So more than proud since you have found it fair.

My lute is ready, and the fragrant drink
    Your lips may honour, how it will rejoice
Losing its life in yours! The lute I think
    But wastes the time when I might hear your voice.

But you desired it, therefore I obey.
    Your slightest, as your utmost, wish or will,
Whether it please you to caress or slay,
    It would please me to give obedience still.

I would delight to die beneath your kiss;
    I envy that young maiden who was slain,
So her warm blood, flowing beneath the kiss,
    Might ease the wounded Sultan of his pain—

If she loved him as I love you, my Lord.
    There is no pleasure on the earth so sweet
As is the pain endured for one adored;
    If I lay crushed beneath your slender feet

I should be happy! Ah, come soon, come soon,
    See how the stars grow large and white above,
The land breeze blows across the salt Lagoon,
    There is no Breeze to cool the heat of love.

Malay Song

The Stars await, serene and white,
  The unarisen moon;
Oh, come and stay with me to-night,
  Beside the salt Lagoon!

My hut is small, but as you lie,
  You see the lighted shore,
And hear the rippling water sigh
  Beneath the pile-raised floor.

No gift have I of jewels or flowers,
  My room is poor and bare:
But all the silver sea is ours,
  And all the scented air

Blown from the mainland, where there grows
  Th' "Intriguer of the Night,"
The flower that you have named Tube-rose,
  Sweet scented, slim, and white.

The flower that, when the air is still
  And no land breezes blow,

From its pale petals can distil
   A phosphorescent glow.

I see your ship at anchor ride;
   Her "captive lightning" shine.
Before she takes to-morrow's tide,
   Let this one night be mine!

Though in the language of your land
   My words are poor and few,
Oh, read my eyes, and understand,
   I give my youth to you!

The Temple Dancing Girl

You will be mine; those lightly dancing feet,
    Falling as softly on the careless street
As the wind-loosened petals of a flower,
    Will bring you here, at the Appointed Hour.

And all the Temple's little links and laws
    Will not for long protect your loveliness.
I have a stronger force to aid my cause,
    Nature's great Law, to love and to possess!

Throughout those sleepless watches, when I lay
    Wakeful, desiring what I might not see,
I knew (it helped those hours, from dusk to day),
    In this one thing, Fate would be kind to me.

You will consent, through all my veins like wine
    This prescience flows; your lips meet mine above,
Your clear soft eyes look upward into mine
    Dim in a silent ecstasy of love.

The clustered softness of your waving hair,
    That curious paleness which enchants me so,

The Temple Dancing Girl

And all your delicate strength and youthful air,
  Destiny will compel you to bestow!

Refuse, withdraw, and hesitate awhile,
  Your young reluctance does but fan the flame;
My partner, Love, waits, with a tender smile,
  Who play against him play a losing game.

I, strong in nothing else, have strength in this,
  The subtlest, most resistless, force we know
Is aiding me; and you must stoop and kiss:
  The genius of the race will have it so!

Yet, make it not too long, nor too intense
  My thirst; lest I should break beneath the strain,
And the worn nerves, and over-wearied sense,
  Enjoy not what they spent themselves to gain.

Lest, in the hour when you consent to share
  That human passion Beauty makes divine,
I, over worn, should find you over fair,
  Lest I should die before I make you mine.

You will consent, those slim, reluctant feet,
  Falling as lightly on the careless street
As the white petals of a wind-worn flower,
  Will bring you here, at the Appointed Hour.

Hira-Singh's Farewell to Burmah

On the wooden deck of the wooden Junk, silent, alone, we lie,
With silver foam about the bow, and a silver moon in the sky:
A glimmer of dimmer silver here, from the anklets round your feet,
Our lips may close on each other's lips, but never our souls may meet.

For though in my arms you lie at rest, your name I have never heard,
To carry a thought between us two, we have not a single word.
And yet what matter we do not speak, when the ardent eyes have spoken,
The way of love is a sweeter way, when the silence is unbroken.

As a wayward Fancy, tired at times, of the cultured Damask Rose,
Drifts away to the tangled copse, where the wild Anemone grows;

So the ordered and licit love ashore, is hardly fresh and free
As this light love in the open wind and salt of the outer sea.

So sweet you are, with your tinted cheeks and your small caressive hands,
What if I carried you home with me, where our Golden Temple stands?
Yet, this were folly indeed; to bind, in fetters of permanence,
A passing dream whose enchantment charms because of its transience.

Life is ever a slave to Time; we have but an hour to rest,
Her steam is up and her lighters leave, the vessel that takes me west;
And never again we two shall meet, as we chance to meet to-night,
On the Junk, whose painted eyes gaze forth, in desolate want of sight.

And what is love at its best, but this? Conceived by a passing glance,
Nursed and reared in a transient mood, on a drifting Sea of Chance.
For rudderless craft are all our loves, among the rocks and the shoals,
Well we may know one another's speech, but never each other's souls.

Give here your lips and kiss me again, we have but a moment more,
Before we set the sail to the mast, before we loosen the oar.
Good-bye to you, and my thanks to you, for the rest you let me share,
While this night drifted away to the Past, to join the Nights that Were.

Starlight

O BEAUTIFUL Stars, when you see me go
   Hither and thither, in search of love,
Do you think me faithless, who gleam and glow
   Serene and fixed in the blue above?
       O Stars, so golden, it is not so.

But there is a garden I dare not see,
   There is a place where I fear to go,
Since the charm and glory of life to me
   The brown earth covered there, long ago.
       O Stars, you saw it, you know, you know.

Hither and thither I wandering go,
   With aimless haste and wearying fret;
In a search for pleasure and love? Not so,
   Seeking desperately to forget.
       You see so many, O Stars, you know.

Sampan Song

A LITTLE breeze blew over the sea,
    And it came from far away,
Across the fields of millet and rice,
All warm with sunshine and sweet with spice,
It lifted his curls and kissed him thrice,
    As upon the deck he lay.

It said, "Oh, idle upon the sea,
    Awake and with sleep have done,
Haul up the widest sail of the prow,
And come with me to the rice fields now,
She longs, oh, how can I tell you how,
    To show you your first-born son!"

Song of the Devoted Slave

THERE is one God: Mahomed his Prophet. Had I his power
I would take the topmost peaks of the snow-clad Himalayas,
And would range them around your dwelling, during the
heats of summer,
To cool the airs that fan your serene and delicate presence,
Had I the power.

Your courtyard should ever be filled with the fleetest of
camels
Laden with inlaid armour, jewels and trappings for horses,
Ripe dates from Egypt, and spices and musk from Arabia.
And the sacred waters of Zem-Zem well, transported
thither,
Should bubble and flow in your chamber, to bathe the
delicate
Slender and wayworn feet of my Lord, returning from
travel,
Had I the power.

Fine woven silk, from the further East, should conceal your
beauty,
Clinging around you in amorous folds; caressive, silken,

Beautiful long-lashed, sweet-voiced Persian boys should, kneeling, serve you,
And the floor beneath your sandalled feet should be smooth and golden,
    Had I the power.

And if ever your clear and stately thoughts should turn to women,
Kings' daughters, maidens, should be appointed to your caresses,
That the youth and the strength of my Lord might never be wasted
In light or sterile love; but enrich the world with his children.
    Had I the power.

Whilst I should sit in the outer court of the Water Palace
To await the time when you went forth, for Pleasure or Warfare,
Descending the stairs rose crowned, or armed and arrayed in purple,—
To mark the place where your steps have fallen, and kiss the footprints,
    Had I the power.

The Singer

The singer only sang the Joy of Life,
    For all too well, alas! the singer knew
How hard the daily toil, how keen the strife,
    How salt the falling tear; the joys how few.

He who thinks hard soon finds it hard to live,
    Learning the Secret Bitterness of Things:
So, leaving thought, the singer strove to give
    A level lightness to his lyric strings.

He only sang of Love; its joy and pain,
    But each man in his early season loves;
Each finds the old, lost Paradise again,
    Unfolding leaves, and roses, nesting doves.

And though that sunlit time flies all too fleetly,
    Delightful Days that dance away too soon!
Its early morning freshness lingers sweetly
    Throughout life's grey and tedious afternoon.

And he, whose dreams enshrine her tender eyes,
    And she, whose senses wait his waking hand,

Impatient youth, that tired but sleepless lies,
  Will read perhaps, and reading, understand.

Oh, roseate lips he would have loved to kiss,
  Oh, eager lovers that he never knew!
What should you know of him, or words of his?—
  But all the songs he sang were sung for you!

Malaria

HE lurks among the reeds, beside the marsh,
    Red oleanders twisted in His hair,
His eyes are haggard and His lips are harsh,
    Upon His breast the bones show gaunt and bare.

The green and stagnant waters lick His feet,
    And from their filmy, iridescent scum
Clouds of mosquitoes, gauzy in the heat,
    Rise with His gifts: Death and Delirium.

His messengers: They bear the deadly taint
    On spangled wings aloft and far away,
Making thin music, strident and yet faint,
    From golden eve to silver break of day.

The baffled sleeper hears th' incessant whine
    Through his tormented dreams, and finds no rest.
The thirsty insects use his blood for wine,
    Probe his blue veins and pasture on his breast.

While far away He in the marshes lies,
    Staining the stagnant water with His breath,

An endless hunger burning in His eyes,
    A famine unassuaged, whose food is Death.

He hides among the ghostly mists that float
    Over the water, weird and white and chill,
And peasants, passing in their laden boat,
    Shiver and feel a sense of coming ill.

A thousand burn and die; He takes no heed,
    Their bones, unburied, strewn upon the plain,
Only increase the frenzy of His greed
    To add more victims to th' already slain.

He loves the haggard frame, the shattered mind,
    Gloats with delight upon the glazing eye,
Yet, in one thing, His cruelty is kind,
    He sends them lovely dreams before they die;

Dreams that bestow on them their heart's desire,
    Visions that find them mad, and leave them blest,
To sink, forgetful of the fever's fire,
    Softly, as in a lover's arms, to rest.

Fancy

FAR in the Further East the skilful craftsman
    Fashioned this fancy for the West's delight.
This rose and azure Dragon, crouching softly
    Upon the satin skin, close-grained and white.

And you lay silent, while his slender needles
    Pricked the intricate pattern on your arm,
Combining deftly Cruelty and Beauty,
    That subtle union, whose child is charm.

Charm irresistible: the lovely something
    We follow in our dreams, but may not reach.
The unattainable Divine Enchantment,
    Hinted in music, never heard in speech.

This from the blue design exhales towards me,
    As incense rises from the Homes of Prayer,
While the unfettered eyes, allured and rested,
    Urge the forbidden lips to stoop and share;

Share in the sweetness of the rose and azure
    Traced in the Dragon's form upon the white
Curve of the arm. Ah, curb thyself, my fancy,
    Where wouldst thou drift in this enchanted flight?

Feroza

THE evening sky was as green as Jade,
 As Emerald turf by Lotus lake,
Behind the Kafila far she strayed,
 (The Pearls are lost if the Necklace break!)

A lingering freshness touched the air
 From palm-trees, clustered around a Spring,
The great, grim Desert lay vast and bare,
 But Youth is ever a careless thing.

The Raiders threw her upon the sand,
 Men of the Wilderness know no laws,
They tore the Amethysts off her hand,
 And rent the folds of her veiling gauze.

They struck the lips that they might have kissed,
 Pitiless they to her pain and fear,
And wrenched the gold from her broken wrist,
 No use to cry; there were none to hear.

Her scarlet mouth and her onyx eyes,
 Her braided hair in its silken sheen,

Feroza

Were surely meet for a Lover's prize,
    But Fate dissented, and stepped between.

Across the Zenith the vultures fly,
    Cruel of beak and heavy of wing.
Thus it was written that she should die.
    Inshallah! Death is a transient thing.

This Month the Almonds Bloom at Kandahar

I HATE this City, seated on the Plain,
  The clang and clamour of the hot Bazar,
Knowing, amid the pauses of my pain,
  This month the Almonds bloom in Kandahar.

The Almond-trees, that sheltered my Delight,
  Screening my happiness as evening fell.
It was well worth—that most Enchanted Night–
  This life in torment, and the next in Hell!

People are kind to me; one More than Kind,
  Her lashes lie like fans upon her cheek,
But kindness is a burden on my mind,
  And it is weariness to hear her speak.

For though that Kaffir's bullet holds me here,
  My thoughts are ever free, and wander far,
To where the Lilac Hills rise, soft and clear,
  Beyond the Almond Groves of Kandahar.

He followed me to Sibi, to the Fair,
    The Horse-fair, where he shot me weeks ago,
But since they fettered him I have no care
    That my returning steps to health are slow.

They will not loose him till they know my fate,
    And I rest here till I am strong to slay,
Meantime, my Heart's Delight may safely wait
    Among the Almond blossoms, sweet as they.

That cursed Kaffir! Well, he won by day,
    But I won, what I so desired, by night,
My arms held what his lack till Judgment Day!
    Also, the game is not yet over—quite!

Wait, Amir Ali, wait till I come forth
    To kill, before the Almond-trees are green,
To raze thy very Memory from the North,
    So that thou art not, and thou hast not been!

Aha! Friend Amir Ali! it is Duty
    To rid the World from Shiah dogs like thee,
They are but ill-placed moles on Islam's beauty,
    Such as the Faithful cannot calmly see!

Also my bullet hurts me not a little,
    Thy Shiah blood might serve to salve the ill.
Maybe some Afghan Promises are brittle;
    Never a Promise to oneself, to kill!

Now I grow stronger, I have days of leisure
 To shape my coming Vengeance as I lie,
And, undisturbed by call of War or Pleasure,
 Can dream of many ways a man may die.

I shall not torture thee, thy friends might rally,
 Some Fate assist thee and prove false to me;
Oh! shouldst thou now escape me, Amir Ali,
 This would torment me through Eternity!

Aye, Shuffa-Jan, I will be quiet indeed,
 Give here the Hakim's powder if thou wilt,
And thou mayst sit, for I perceive thy need,
 And rest thy soft-haired head upon my quilt.

Thy gentle love will not disturb a mind
 That loves and hates beneath a fiercer Star.
Also, thou know'st, my Heart is left behind,
 Among the Almond-trees of Kandahar!

Stars of the Desert

To Aziz: Song of Mahomed Akram

Your beauty puts a barb into my soul,
    Strive as I will it never lets me go.
My love has passed the frontiers of control,
    You are so fair and I desire you so.

Others may come and go, they are to me
    But changing mirage, transient, untrue,
My faithlessness is but fidelity
    Since I am never faithful, but to you.

You are not kind to me, but many are
    And all their kindness does not make them dear;
It may be you deceive me when afar
    Even as always you torment me near.

Yet is your beauty so divine a thing,
    So irreplaceable, so haunting sweet
Against all reason, I am fain to fling
    My life, my youth, myself, beneath your feet.

Surf Song

My little one, come and listen
    To the calling of the sea,
And watch how the wet sands glisten
    Where the surf has left them free.
As thou and the wind together
    Shall frolic along the strand;
Thy feet as light as a feather
    Will hardly dent the sand.
Unwind the veils that enfold thee,
    Thou never wast shy with me;
The sea will rejoice to hold thee,
    The stars will delight to see.
The beauty thou shalt discover,
    Oh, Morning Star of my heart,
Will dazzle even thy lover
    Who knows how fair thou art!

Oh, Life, I Have Taken You for My Lover!

(To Arthus E. J. Legge, who suggested this idea)

Oh, Life, I have taken you for my Lover,
   I rent your veils and I found you fair;
If a fault or failing my eyes discover,
   I will not see it; it is not there!

I know, *if I knew*, I should hold you dearer,
   Should understand, *if I understood*,
For I worship more, as you draw me nearer,
   Your reckless Evil, your perfect Good.

In the Jungle gloom, we have watched and waited,
   For stealthy Panthers, that prowl by night,
At the end of some weary march, belated,
   We heard strange tales by the camp-fire light.

We have lain on the starlit sands, untented,
   While low-hung planets rose white and fair,
And in moonlit gardens, silver and scented,
   Oh, Life, my Lover, how sweet you were!

Forbidden and barbarous rites were shown us,
　In rock-hewn Temples and jungle caves,
And the smoke-wreathed home of the dead has known us,—
　The burning-ghat by the Ganges' waves.

Ah, the long, lone ride through the starlit hours,
　The long, lone watch on the starlit sea,
And the flame and flush of the morning flowers
　When Life, my Lover, was kind to me!

Betimes we were out on the Sea, together;
　The vessel raced down the great green slope
Of mountainous waves, in desperate weather;
　The hearts of men were adrift from hope.

As over the deck, in exultant fashion,
　The violent water crashed and fell,
I knew, through the joy of your reckless passion,
　Agonized fear of the last farewell.

But I follow you always, unresisting,
　To lowest depth; to uttermost brink,
From a thirst like mine there is no desisting
　Though given poison for wine to drink.

You may do your utmost, you will not shake me,
　Your faith may falter; my faith is true.

Oh, Life, you may shatter and rend and break me,
  All Pain is Pleasure, that springs from you!

In the height and heat of your wildest passion,
  You had your uttermost will of me,
And when have I asked for the least compassion?
  A lover loved is a lover free!

Though, with never a word of farewell spoken
  In lonely wilds of some Desert place,
You have flung me from you, adrift and broken
  To wait the child of your last embrace.

And never my faith nor my fervour faltered,
  Until you turned to my lips again,
When, my eager longing for you unaltered
  Your first kiss cancelled my months of pain.

Ah, Life, you may torture my soul, betray me,
  The right is yours, as Lover and Lord.
And when in the climax of all, you slay me,
  My lips in dying will seek your sword.

Illusion

Thinking you had a heart that love could break,
A lovely gentle soul that might awake,
I held you tenderly for either's sake,
   And showed you nothing but love's ecstasy.

Now, though you have no heart to melt or burn,
No soul to wonder, meditate or yearn,
Your beauty is a fact; lie still and learn
   Something of passionate love's intensity.

Sleep

(The Moorish Slave, at Fidala, Morocco)

There is something so beseeching in the attitude of sleep,
  A pathetic resignation, most appealing to the heart.
There must surely be some secret that the eyes in slumber keep,
  Which the lips, on their awakening, could not, if they would impart.

See yon Slave from Sus, recumbent, with his ebon arms outspread
  On the marigold he crushes to a sheet of golden flowers,
How the mystery of dreaming lends a halo to his head,
  And exalts him to a level never reached in waking hours.

In the form that lies impassive, while the sea-wind comes and goes
  And uplifts his rags in pity, on its cool refreshing breath,
There is something so prophetic of the Last and Great Repose:
  Sleep has borrowed, in its quietude, the Dignity of Death.

Though his parted lips are wordless, though he breathes no uttered prayer

Yet his silence seems imploring, "Let me deem the noon-
     day night,
For my dreams are velvet-breasted, and they shelter me
     from care,
I entreat thee not to wake me to the sorrows of the light."

Ah, sleep on, in peace, my brother, to awaken when thou
     wilt,
From the dreams that treat thee kindly, and the rest that
     sets thee free.
With the wild fig for thy canopy, the marigolds thy quilt,
And, to serve thee for a lullaby, the thunder of the Sea.

Song of the Enfifa River
(In memory of Abdullah, drowned at sixteen, on
the road to Rabat, Morocco)

At day-break, when the tide was low
   He came to bathe his slender feet,
And laughing, sported to and fro,
   Across my waters cool and sweet.

Obedient to his Faith's decree
   His sable hair was shorn away,
One curl was left, that floating free,
   I longed to deck with silver spray.

His eyes were wide and full of light,
   Young eyes, where dreams and fancies glow.
There was no star in Heaven so bright,
   And I reflect the stars, and know.

He gave himself to my embrace,
   Ah, Youth, confiding and unwise!
My kisses clustered on his face;
   How should I render up my prize?

Yet he withdrew; my waves were weak.
    He loitered on my banks awhile,
Shook my caresses from his cheek,
    And left me with a careless smile.

I let him leave; my tides were low.
    But, seeking succour of the Sea
At noon I felt the breakers flow
    Across the bar, and join with me.

I waited in the heat; at length
    Again he came to bathe alone,
Then, in the fulness of my strength,
    I caught and held him for my own!

His strong young arms apart he flung,
    His red lips cried, I had no care.
In eddies round his limbs I clung,
    And rippled in and out his hair.

I bore him downwards to the Sea,
    The white surf met us on the sand,
His beauty was made one with me
    Who saw and loved it on the land.

I laid him down upon the bar,
    Played with his hair, and kissed his eyes.
How cold those mortal lovers are!
    He sleeps and makes me no replies.

My tides run low; he will not wake,
   His hands drift, like an empty shell.
I stole him for his beauty's sake,
   Alas, Enfifa did not well!

His young lips show no stir of breath.
   Ah,—I begin to understand,
And I remember:—this is Death!
   The haunting terror of the land.

The River of Pearls at Fez: Translation

ONE evening we sat together
By the River of Pearls at Fez,
Stringing verses and sometimes singing.
My gaze followed the beautiful boy
Who, with a swift and delicate movement,
Flung the wine-cup over his shoulder;
The ruby drops glittered and fell
Bright in the dying sunshine.
The River of Pearls shone like a sword in the grass,
Not disdaining
The work of turning the waterwheel,
And the sun, reluctant, lingered about the tree-tops
In a golden mist of farewell.

Many the tears that have fallen since,
Many the nights that have passed,
But I remembered
The River of Pearls at Fez
And Seomar whom I loved.

Syed Amir

SYED AMIR is dead, and his numerous foes
Are hushed in breathless awe of amazed relief.
The hearts of his friends are cold as the Tirah snows,
And I am blind and deaf in the Grip of my Grief.
My Soul has borrowed a portion of Pain from Hell.
Oh, Syed Amir, my Brother and Friend, Farewell!

His women weep, but a woman's tears flow lightly.
A bauble or two, or a child, can soon console.
But I, who am strange to tears, lie sleepless, nightly,
Feeling the Fangs of Grief in my desolate soul.
I maddened myself with *Churus,* it could not cure me—
Ransacked the Bazar, to beg at the hands of lust
An hour's respite, but how was sin to allure me,
Who know the beauty of Syed Amir is dust?

A little while I wander in Tribulation,
In a Feud or two, or a few light loves take part,
But Death will come, and this is my Consolation,
Men live not long with a stricken and wounded heart.
What further challenge from Fate can I hope or fear,
Who mourn the ruined glory of Syed Amir?

All gifts were Syed Amir's; an Arrestive Beauty
That caught men's breath when he passed, Serene and Royal,
A clear and delicate Mind, where Honour and Duty
Sentried the gate, that nothing might pass disloyal,
And these are taken from Khorassan for ever,
Their light is quenched in the land where he used to dwell,
But I, who loved him, cease from loving him never,
Oh, Syed Amir, my Brother and Friend, Farewell!

Au Salon

A sky intensely blue, a low, white wall,
Against it heaps of up-blown yellow sand,
A sleeping figure, holding in her hand
Some scarlet cactus blossom; that was all.
And yet so mellowly the sunbeams fell
Upon the sunburnt limbs, such subtle play
Of rosy light and tender shadow lay
Upon the upturned face, that all could tell
An artist painted with a poet's eyes;
And warmly an enthusiastic glow
Ran through the groups that criticised below
While one, who gazed with pleasure and surprise
Said, and I do not think he said amiss,
"He was her lover when he painted this!"

The Lute Player of Casa Blanca

No others sing as you have sung,
   Oh, Well Beloved of me!
So glad you are, so lithe and young,
   As joyous as the sea,
That dances in the golden rain
   The falling sunbeams fling,—
Ah, stoop and kiss me once again
   Then take your lute and sing.
      Oh, Lute player, my Lute player,
      Take up your lute and sing!

The wind comes blowing, light and free:
   In all the summer isles
No laughing thing is found to see
   As brilliant as your smiles.
You are the very heart of Youth,
   The very Soul of Song,
That lovely dream, made living truth,
   For which the poets long.
      Oh, Lute player, my Lute player,
      The very Soul of Song!

Ah, dear and dark-eyed Lute player,
    This joy is almost pain,
To reach, when evening cools the air,
    Your level roof again.
To see the palms, erect and slim,
    Against a golden sky,
And hear, as twilight closes dim,
    The Mouddin's mournful cry,
        Across your songs, my Lute player,
        The Faithful's evening cry.

Each slender finger lightly slips
    To its appointed strings,
Ah, the sweet scarlet, parted lips
    Of One Beloved, who sings!
Ah, the soft radiance of eyes
    By love and music lit!
What need of Heaven beyond the skies
    Since here we enter it?
        You make my Heaven, my Lute player,
        And hold the keys of it!

And when the music waxes strong
    I hear the sound of War,
The drums are throbbing in the song,
    The clamour and the roar.
The Desert's self is in the strain,
    The agony of slaves,

The winds that sigh, as if in pain,
   About forgotten graves,
     Oh, Lute player, my Lute player,
   Those lonely Desert graves!

The sightless sockets, whence the eyes
   Were wrenched or burnt away,
The mangled form that ere it dies,
   Becomes the jackals' prey,
The forced caress, the purchased smile,
   Ere youth be yet awake,—
Ah, break your melody awhile
   Or else my heart will break!
     I sometimes think, my Lute player,
   You wish my heart to break!

The sunset fires desert the West,
   The stars invade the sky,
Lover of mine, 'tis time to rest
   And let the music die.
Though Melody awake the morn,
   Yet Love should end the day.
I kiss your hand the strings have worn
   And take your lute away.
     I kiss your hand, my Lute player,
   And take the Lute away.

At twilight on this roof of ours,
   So lonely and so high,

We catch the scent of all the flowers
    Ascending to the sky.
Sultan of Song, whose burning eyes
    Outblaze the stars above,
Forget not, when the sunset dies
    You reign as Lord of Love!
        Ah, come to me, my Lute player,
        Lover, and Lord of Love!

The Hospital on the Shore

THE youthful swimmers come up on the beach,
　Naked and fresh from the kiss of the sea,
I hear the sound of their light-hearted speech;
　As it is with them, it was once with me!
　　Oh, Death, grant me pity: just one day **more,**
　　And let me go down again to the shore.

I could have died in the rush of the air,
　Mid crashing water and petulant spray,
The surf in my teeth, the wind in my hair,
　Rejoicing, exultant, even as they.
　　But to meet Death here, . . . in this walled-in **cage,**
　　I am dumb with terror and blind with rage.

Have pity! Reprieve me! just one more ride,
　White sand beneath us, white planets above,
One last long sail with the ebb of the tide,
　One lilac evening of delicate love.
　　One lingering look at those eyes of his.
　　To remember through the Eternities.

Among the Sandhills

Lie still, Beloved, I also see the day
    Shoot his white arrows through the trembling sky,
But what is dawn to us, who cast away
    All sense of time that mars our ecstasy?

The scented orange bushes check the breeze,
    Granting in tribute many waxen stars,
And aromatic Eucalyptus trees
    Defy the sun with grey-green scimitars.

Since fate has given us this garden love,
    And Time and Space, for once, have acquiesced,
Ah, take no heed of paling skies above,
    Let us deem night is with us yet, and rest.

Let us lie still and drift away in dreams,
    Back to the jewelled kingdom of the night,
Whose golden stars with dimly radiant gleams
    Lit up your loveliness for my delight.

Once we are risen all the cares of day
    Will seize and bind us to their wanton will.
Why should we own that night has passed away?
    Oh, as you value love, lie still, lie still!

The Cactus

THE scarlet flower, with never a sister leaf,
    Stemless, springs from the edge of the Cactus-thorn:
Thus from the ragged wounds of desperate grief
    A beautiful Thought, perfect and pure, is born.

Lalla Radha and the Churel

His sixteen years had left him very fair,
   Tinted his cheeks with soft and delicate bloom,
Added new lustre to his clustered hair,
   And filled his amber eyes with tender gloom.

He sought some unknown thing, he knew not what,
   His scarce-seen bride, a child, was far away,
Desiring love, as yet he knew it not,
   Sleepless by night he grew, forlorn by day.

Priest

"Ah, go not near the Peepul trees,
That shiver in the evening breeze,
A young Churel might hide in these!

"And should she see thee, and desire,
Then will she burn thee in soft fire,
Till in her arms thou shalt expire!"

Lalla Radha

"But who and what is this Churel,
Who loves in Peepul trees to dwell,

    The Peepul, where the Koel sings
    In frenzied songs, of amorous things?"

Priest

"When, with her child unborn, a woman dies,
Her spirit takes the form of a Churel,
A maiden's form, with soft, alluring eyes,
Where promises of future rapture dwell.
    Yet is her loveliness, though passing sweet,
    Marred by the backward turning of her feet.

"She sits in branches of the Peepul trees,
Until beneath, a passing youth she sees.
Should she desire him, swift, she will alight,
Entreating softly 'Stay with me to-night!'
    No safety then for him; unless he flies,
    Soon, in the furnace of her love, he dies!"

Lalla Radha

"But if indeed these things are so,
    Yet what am I, that she should care,
To watch me as I pass below,
    Or notice me and find me fair?"

Priest

"Yours are the happiest gifts that the Gods have given,
Who have never been over ready with gifts to part.

Youth, the divine reminiscence of some lost Heaven,
  Beauty, the dream of the eyes, the desire of the heart.

"Beauty, that women adore and secretly pray for,
  To find, to possess, to bequeath to the world again,
The loveliest stake that Life allows them to play for,
  At the risk of death; with certain foreknowledge of pain."

> DANCING GIRL (*singing in the distance*)
>
> "What will you do with your seventeenth year,
>   You with the eyes of a dove?
> Give it to Love, he will hold you lightly,
> Betray you and wound you more than slightly,
> But lead you into Paradise nightly,
>   Give it to Love!!"

He heard and waited awhile, but the days flew by,
And brought a more brilliant sun to the azure sky.

The scent of the flowers grew stronger, grew keen as pain,
And Youth's sweet ferment rose from his heart to his brain

Until, when the west was red, and the evening breeze
Broke fresh on his lips, he went to the Peepul trees.

> SONG OF THE CHUREL
>
> "Ah, come to me, I want you so!
> Why will you make me wait?
> The golden sunsets burn and glow,

The twilight moments come and go,
I watch you wander to and fro,
   Why do you hesitate?

"So very brief Youth's season is,
   Ah, wherefore waste a single night?
Put up your lips for mine to kiss,
   Take the first promise of delight.

"Upon Life's pale and tragic face,
   Youth passes like a blush.
It blooms, an evanescent grace,
Alas, for such a little space,
And fading, hardly leaves a trace,
   Of all its radiant flush.

"We cannot force one night to last,
   Or stay a single star at will,
And though the Pulse of Youth is fast,
   The Wings of Time are swifter still.

"So much I want your silken hair,
   Your youth, intact and free,
A thousand nights, serenely fair,
With scented silence everywhere,
Consenting stars and pliant air,
   Would pass too soon for me.

"Too soon the rising flood of morn
   Our isle of night would overflow,

And force upon our eyes forlorn
 Its lovely but unwanted glow.

"The magic Garden of Delight
 Is ours; I hold the key.
Take up Love's sceptre, yours by right,
And learn his mystery and might,
Ah, come and reign with me to-night,
 In silent ecstasy!

"Come, while the silver stars above
 Rain down their light serene and still,
And if you cannot come for love,
 Ah, come on any terms you will!"

. . . . .

How should the youth resist, deny,
 Or turn his lips from hers away?
Nightly, beneath th' unheeding sky,
 The fierce Churel caressed her prey.

Nightly, the flickering Peepul trees
 Echoed his soft and broken sighs,
While the faint eddies of the breeze
 In pity fanned his sleepless eyes.

Frailer he grew, more wan and pale,
 Possession only fed Desire,
Like wax he felt his forces fail,
 Consumed in her insistent fire.

Till lost in dreams, his fainting breath
    Shed on her lips in one last sigh,
He neither knew nor noticed death.
    This is the loveliest way to die!

Beneath the Peepuls dead he lay,
    Pale on his face the starlight fell,
In ecstasy he passed away.
    Such is the love of the Churel.

Rabat: Morocco

Oh, walled, white City, rising from the plain,
  Between the grey-green grass, the grey-blue skies,
How we have longed for you, and watched in vain
  Till your pale beauty rose upon our eyes.

From Orange groves, beyond your gated walls,
  Faint scents of Citron bloom float far away.
Upon each wind-worn face the perfume falls
  Till we forget the journey of the day.

Forget the weary march, its dust and heat,
  The frequent carrion that taints the air,
The three-inch spur, the lame and stumbling feet,
  The pointed stirrup, clogged with blood and hair.

Forget the wretched brute, that strains and strives,
  Staggers a few more paces with his load
Then falls and dies, beneath the open knives,
  The kicks and curses of the savage road.

Let us forget (in such forgetfulness
  Lies the one chance, perhaps, of life at all!)

While our burnt lips receive the soft caress
    Exhaled from Orange flowers beyond the wall.

Ah, sea-set City, grant my heart's request!
    Where your slim minarets soar white above
Your fragrant Orange gardens, grant me rest,
    And from some child of yours, a little love.
        Ah, walled, white City, grant me a little love!

Gathered from Ternina's Face
(To N. L. K. in memory of June 23rd)

Tristan, oh, Tristan! Death has set us free!
There is no barrier now, 'twixt me and thee,
For Fate allows my lips their "come to me"!!
Tristan!

We, from this night, no more of night shall know;
For us, no paling stars, no dawning glow;
Ah, I am more than glad to have it so,
Tristan!

I feared the poison, now I feel the thrill
Through all my veins like liquid fire, and still
It brings no pain, nor any sense of ill,
Tristan!

Only a tender, strange desire for thee,
While the winged moments perish silently.
Ah, come, lest Death forestall thee, come to me,
Tristan!

Most gracious Death, who sets me free to speak;
He strengthens me, who makes all others weak,

Brings blushes and no pallor to my cheek,
>   Tristan!

Listen; I say the words I could not say
Had we to rise and meet another day,
But in the falling shades of Death, I may!
>   Tristan!

There will be no to-morrow; I shall keep
Tristan for ever in my arms asleep.
Not even dreams will share a rest so deep,
>   Tristan!

My face will be the last face thou shalt see.
Thy spirit, entering on Eternity,
Will pause to take an ultimate kiss from me,
>   Tristan!

Ah, come to me, since Death has given the right.
I love thee so, I could have died to-night
Without the poison's aid, from sheer delight,
>   Tristan!

Much may be done by those about to die,
Much may be said by lips that say "Good-bye,"
On which the Last Great Silence soon must lie,
>   Tristan!

With Death to shelter me, I greatly dare,
My lips seek things mine eyes have long found fair,
This is thy mouth,—and this, thy falling hair,
                        Tristan!

Thy falling hair,—so soft upon my brow,
Never a lover has been loved as thou!
If this is Death, I have not lived till now!
                        Tristan!

Opium: Li's Riverside Hut at Taku

THE room is bare, the paper windows shiver,
    Beneath the ill-hung door, the sleet blows free,
Yet here, Delight flows forth, a gentle river,
    To saturate my soul with ecstasy!

I lie upon the heated *Kang*, quiescent,
    Lulled by the warmth of lighted straw below,
While Li, the golden-tinted adolescent,
    Blue-clad and silent, passes to and fro.

Li, with his well-cut lips and supple fingers,
    His crudely lidded eyes, that seem to gaze
Back through ten thousand years of thought, where lingers
    Some misty splendour of the old, old days.

Free from the plait, his loosened sable tresses
    In silken waves, below the knee, descend.
Bringing the opium pipe, he deftly presses
    The viscous drug upon the needle's end.

Lights it, inserts it in the pipe beside me,
    Then through my lips the magic vapour streams,

And Life and Love, that seldom satisfied me,
    Meet me with lovely faces in my dreams.

Life at his brightest, flushed and crowned with flowers,
    Brings gifts no mortal, waking, e'er possessed,
Exquisite Chances, and Enchanted Hours,
    While Love,—Love brings me you, to share my rest!

In the Water Palace

The gracious rain caressed the fields
  To bountiful increase,
Profusion reigned throughout the land,
  And, on the borders, peace.

Yet, in the streets, the people cried,
  "It is a shameful thing,
Now all the Gods are more than kind,
  This madness of the King."

A gipsy-girl his heart ensnares,
  And all his days and nights
Are spent, unmindful of the State,
  In profitless delights.

The Maharani sits alone,
  Her lashes wet with tears,
While all the pearls and gems of state
  Her gipsy rival wears.

In vain they bring her silken robes,
  In vain her maidens sing,
She will but sigh, "When shall I see
  The beauty of the king?"

The gipsy's youth is all but o'er,
  Her time for children past,
The people say, "Without a son
  How shall the kingdom last?"

And louder yet the murmurs grow,
  O folly and disgrace,
And faster still the Rani's tears
  Flow down her youthful face.

One night, a faithful handmaiden
  Unto her chamber came;
"Presence," she said, " 'tis thou alone
  Canst save the king from shame.

"The gipsy girl we drugged to-night
  And stole her silks away,
Rise thou, and play the wanton's part
  Until the dawn of day.

"We gave a philtre to the king
  To set his brain afire,
And thou shalt take the gipsy's place
  To solace his desire.

"Thus lying joyous on thy heart,
  If all propitious be,
He, thinking of the gipsy's charms,
  Shall bring a son to thee.

"If this, oh, Rani, thou canst do
  Thy virtue will be great;
Thou from himself wilt save the king,
  And from the king the state.

"But ah, remember, he must go
  Before the skies grow light,
Ere yet the philtre leave his brain
  Too clear in sense and sight.

"For should he dream that thou art thou,
  And realise the truth
Too suddenly, he would not spare
  Thy beauty or thy youth.

"In some auspicious, later hour,
  If our desire be gained,
The tender sequence of the fraud
  To him can be explained."

The Maharani rose and smiled,
  She pushed her hair away,
"Ah, if he stay with me to-night,
  At daybreak let him slay!"

Then round her slender neck she twined
  The pearls as white as milk;
Her breast was all too young to fill
  The crimson bodice silk.

She blushed to wear the gipsy's robes,
   And yet they seemed to bring
A subtle sweetness to her soul,
   Since well they knew the king.

And "Ah," she said, "I love him so,
   I tremble with delight;
Would that I knew the gipsy's spell
   To charm him through the night!"

Then to her rival's bower she went,
   (Who far, unconscious, lay,)
And waited in a flush of joy
   Till he should pass that way.

He came in all his jewelled state,
   His dagger by his side,
The philtre filled him with desire
   Fierce to be satisfied.

His youth and beauty changed her love
   To passion at its best,
And round his neck she wound her arms
   And took him to her breast.

She was so sweet, she loved so well,
   Before the night was past,
He murmured, "Ah, my gipsy queen,
   Thou lovest me at last!"

The watchful woman by the door
    Waited in hope and fear,
Praying the Gods that all go well
    For her she held so dear.

And when the night had somewhat waned,
    And sleep had closed his eyes,
"Presence," she said, "unclasp thine arms
    And bid thy lover rise."

The little Rani held him close
    And smiling answered low,
"My lover is so sweet to me
    I cannot let him go."

And once again she came to warn;
    The Rani begged reprieve,
"Love is so sweet and new to me
    How can I let him leave?"

A third time came the handmaiden,
    Sleep weighted both their eyes,
The Rani sighed, "I love him so,
    I cannot bid him rise!"

Thus all three slept until the dawn
    Rose tremulous and clear,
And soon the sunlight through the room
    Pierced like a golden spear.

It struck the king across the eyes,
    He rose alert and keen,
He saw the pearls he knew so well,
    But not the gipsy queen.

The Rani waking, held him still,
    He tore her arms apart.
"This for thy treachery," he cried,
    And stabbed her through the heart.

The Crucifix

Oh, slender Christ, upon the Cross before me,
    Whose wistful eyes are sad and shaped for tears,
What have we done, of all that you commanded?
    Little enough! these last two thousand years.

Should any soul be touched with grace or glory,
    Surely such gifts are their possessor's loss:
Hemlock to Socrates, the stake for Bruno,
    And, to your young Divinity, the Cross.

That Cross, on which you hung, serene and dying,
    Until the last, to your own tenets true,
Praying amid your long drawn torments, "Father
    Forgive them, for they know not what they do."

Forgive, *forgive* us, for our senseless folly,
    After these weary centuries, who *can?*
We, who relinquished priceless consolation,
    That else those tender lips had left for Man.

Ours was the cruelty, the wasteful madness,
    And ours, alas, th' irrevocable loss,
You touched our languished world with gentle solace,
    And in return, we gave you to the Cross!

Wind o' the Waste:
On the Wall of Pekin

The icy wind sweeps over the desolate snows,
   Over the Desert of Gobi, towards the sea.
I envy this headless corpse, for it sleeps and knows
   No more of our human life and its agony.

He was a robber when living, and scaled the wall
   To escape his foes, (Ah, could one escape from love)
They would have flayed him alive had he chanced to fall
   Into their hands, so he strangled himself above.

And after a while the body rotted and fell,
   The head still hangs on the nail by the broken stair,
Wherever his soul is now, it has left the Hell
   That passion makes for us here of hate and despair.

Alas, this land of cruel and desolate things!
   How can the Roses of Happiness come to bloom,
Or that butterfly, Love, flutter his silken wings,
   While the bitter wind of the waste lashes the gloom?

Happiness

"Nothing succeeds as doth succeed Success!"
None who have known Success assent to this.

Have I not kissed beloved, consenting lips,
And through my kisses cursed their sweet consent?
Turning my face towards the desert stars
To pray the chillness of the midnight breeze
Might cool the passion that demanded mine.

And all the Gold, wrenched from the stubborn rock,
The utmost Glory, gathered on the Field,
When have they proved a lure to Happiness?

Happiness is so reticent and shy,
So transient, so illusive, and so young,
Most men but glimpse her through the morning flowers,
Or the faint mirage of a passing dream.

She meets her lovers on the summer seas,
Among the shadows of the quiet hills,
Grants them, perchance, a moment's ecstasy,
Then, ere they realise her, she is gone.

Dreamers of Dreams arrest her wayward steps,
And to the Young her kindest kiss is given.
But none have claimed the maiden for a bride,
Set her obedient by the daily hearth,
Or raised a child of theirs from happiness.

Happiness to Success is as a rose,
Perfumed and dewy, in a nest of leaves,
Is to a carven gem of emerald
Circling a ruby on a golden stem.

Take thou the jewel, Friend, and let me lose
What soul I have, among the Lotus flowers!

The Orange Garden

(Translation from the Moorish by Walter Harris
of Tangier)

I

I cannot find this Orange Garden fair:
　　The dim dishevelled grass is wet and chill.
Desolate, croaking frogs distress the air,
　　But birds, if ever birds come here, are still.

Even the oranges have lost their light
　　And droop forlorn beneath the sombre green.
A water-wheel creaks somewhere out of sight,
　　Grey mist and shadow veil the lonely scene.

And when I think I hear your coming feet
　　Rustle across the grass and violet leaves,
'Tis but the gardener, who fears to meet,
　　Among the gloom some fruit-attracted thieves.

II

Fair, ah, fair, is the sunny Orange Garden,
　　Secret and shady, scented and green.

Gold, red gold, are the oranges in clusters,
    Fragrant and bright in their ripened sheen.

Even the croaking of the frogs is music,
    Even the creak of the wheel is song,
Straight to my naked heart the wild birds' warble
    Strikes in cadence, tremulously strong.

Now the old gardener passes discreetly,
    Never upraising his guarded eyes,
For here in the violets, at rest, beside me,
    Sweet and consenting, my Loved One lies!

Droit du Seigneur

The Aspens shiver by the osier bed,
    The waters ripple in September's sun
Among the rushes, where I sit and dream
    My basket empty and my work undone.

I watch the spirals of blue smoke arise
    Above the green of oak and chestnut tree;
Only one week of wistful weariness
    Before as custom bids, I go to thee.

But, wilt thou take thy right? My brother's wife
    Went to the castle on her wedding-day,
And when thou saw'st her shivering dissent
    Didst thou not say in kindness, "Go thy way,

"Untouched by me, even as thou hast come,
    Save in the way of gifts; take this and this."
And she, poor little fool, rejoined her mate,
    Unharmed, *unhonoured*, even by a kiss.

Last week I saw her at her cottage door
    Nursing her clumsy child; no wistful sigh
For what her peasant arms might yet have held,
    A child of thine—broke her serenity.

Ah, if I knew how thou wilt deal with me.
    Who knows? who knows? They tell me I am fair,
And any beauty that I may possess
    Have I not kept it for thy sake with care?

To guard a pallor that might blush for thee,
    Shading the sunrays from this face of mine,
Smoothing my hands with milk from elder-flowers
    Lest the rough skin should jar the silk of thine.

Ah, how I loved thee, even as a child
    Watching thee ride across the village square,
The curls blown backwards from thy vivid face,
    Thy pennons lifted on the summer air.

How I have envied brides who passed thy gates,
    And when I heard the village gossips say
Thou wert not as thy fathers; oft refused
    To claim thy privilege, turned away

So glad and yet so sad,—it well may be
    They will not notice me, those eyes of thine;
Yet surely love will find some soft appeal
    To draw their gaze to me, thy lips to mine.

My cousin loves me; in his kindly eyes
    Lies the clear promise of a calm content.
I, wedding him, ensure his happiness
    As thou ensurest mine, shouldst thou consent.

Ah, if thou shouldst be kind and set thy seal
    On me and mine for ever. Women know
The secret ways of love and all its lore
    If,—ah, dear God in Heaven, if this were so!

My firstborn should be thine, then all my life
    Will, and must, keep the memory of thee.
Even as thou art printed on my heart,
    So on my being must thy impress be.

No second lover and no second child
    Efface the imprint of the first who came,
And on the golden sands of youth inscribed
    Lightly, but so indelibly, his name.

Many a custom, many an old abuse
    Thy people cherish still, unknown to thee;
My cousin whispers me among the reeds,
    "What has the priest to do with thee and me?

"Let us forestall our marriage, thus thy child
    Will be thy husband's, not a lawless thing
Born of injustice." Ah, how blind men are,
    How strange their words of careless kindness ring.

It is the sweetest justice of our lives
    That once, ere settling to our lifelong task
Of serving boors and raising sons to them
    One golden moment, too divine to ask

In our most daring prayers, is flung to us
   By our time honoured custom's strange decree,
One perfect hour of radiant romance
   Is lent to us; will it be lent to me?

Rarely men understand our way of love;
   How that to women in their wedding hours
Lover and priest and king are blent in one,
   Hence the awed worship of these hearts of ours.

At times love for a little lifts the veil
   And men and women see each other's heart
But swiftly passion comes, obscuring all,
   And thus the nearing souls are swept apart.

To us love is a sacred rite; to men
   Custom, perhaps affection, or desire.
Before we hold our lovers in our arms
   They are too fiercely amorous to inquire.

And after too indifferent; thus our souls
   Remain an unread chapter to the end,
And those whose very life is blent with ours
   Cannot be called with justice even friend.

Ah me, I dream and dream: my basket lies
   Unfilled beside me, while the aspens part
Their trembling leaves, and show the castle walls
   That rest my eyes and draw my anxious heart,

Because they hold its treasure. Ah, Seigneur,
  So loved, so longed for, passing strange it seems
That I shall speak to thee, to whom I speak
  Daily in thought, and nightly through my dreams.

Thou may'st misunderstand. Excess of love
  Takes the pale lips of coldness or of art.
And yet my eyes must surely find some way
  To show the white heat burning at my heart!

Seigneur, not so dissimilar am I
  From thee and thine. Thou know'st thy father's ways,
Aye, and his father's; much the castle blood
  Mixed with the village stream in former days.

Signs of more brilliant lineage than my own
  Many have marked in me. Take heed of this;
Find me not too unworthy of thine arms;
  These lips are thine knowing no other kiss.

Think; if thou givest me an hour's delight
  It will be all my life will ever know.
Seigneur, have pity on this love of mine
  And lend thyself to me before I go

Back to my narrow life. The whitest star
  May let its pure and trembling beauty rest
In the dim silver of the smallest pool;
  Wherefore not thou a moment on my breast?

I am thine own by immemorial right,
    Stoop thou and take that privilege of thine;
An hour's dalliance in thy life, Seigneur,
    And an eternal memory in mine!

Korean Song

"Ah, paddle not thou afar from shore
  Where the Great Stream meets the sea,
The River Pirates will snatch thy gold
  And beat out thy life from thee."
      "But thine eyes, my Beloved, thine eyes,
        Have they no peril for me?"

"Ah, go not down to the dens by night
  Where they sell thee poppied dreams,
Like evil eyes, through the spiral smoke,
  The lighted opium gleams."
      "What of thine eyes, oh, my Beloved,
        Have they no alluring beams?"

"Ah, stray not where last year's Lotus stalks
  Are gripped in the frozen mere,
The treacherous ice is over thin."
    "It is not the ice I fear,
      But thine eyes, my Beloved, thine eyes,
        So dangerous and so dear!"

Stars of the Desert
(Mahomed Akram's Night Watch)

*T*HE night is calm, and all the stars are burning,
   Around our camp the sands stretch far away,
No sound, except the lonely jackals howling,
   Until the horses, startled, wake and neigh.

Only the walls of one thin tent of canvas,
   Only a yard of yellow desert sand,
Between us two, and yet I know you distant,
   As though you lived in some far Northern land.

Here, at the doorway of my tent, I linger
   To watch in yours the shadow and the light,
The hungry soul within me burning, burning,
   As the stars burn throughout the Eastern night.

I know well how you sleep, your head thrown backwards,
   Your loose hair ruffled up and disarrayed,
Your fervent eyes still sombre in their slumber
   From the dark circle of the lashes' shade.

I listen to your even cadenced breathing,
   From the soft curve of parted lips set free;

Only a slender wall of wind-stirred canvas
    Between your loveliness asleep and me.

Sleep on, I sit and watch your tent in silence,
    White as a sail upon this sandy sea,
And know the Desert's self is not more boundless
    Than is the distance 'twixt yourself and me.

Know that I am some low red planet burning.
    You in the Zenith, a serene white star,
And I to you, less than the lonely jackals
    That howl among the sandy wastes afar.

Sleep on, the Desert sleeps around you, quiet,
    Watched by the restless, golden stars above,
Ay, let us sleep; you to your careless waking,
    I, with my dreams of unrequited love.

The Fisherman's Bride

The great grey waves, with an angry moan,
    Rush in on the patient sand.
The spray from their crests is backwards blown
    By the strong wind from the land.

As curls are blown from a maiden's face
    And flutter behind her free,
The spindrift blows from the waves that race
    From stress of the outer sea.

The restless wind has ever a sigh
    And the waves are salt as tears,
Maybe because of the dead who lie
    Where never the sunlight peers.

One curl of his hair is more to me
    Than a thousand waves of thine,
Yet is his life in thy charge, oh, sea,
    And also and therefore mine.

Great sins are written against thy name
    In records of olden times.

Art thou not filled with sorrow and shame
   Remembering ancient crimes?

Then spare, oh, spare this lover of mine,
   Thou queen of a million ships,
Content thee with that coral of thine
   And leave me my lover's lips!

The End

In the past I have craved for many a thing.
    And ever you answered "No,"
Now I would ask you for one thing more;
    For God's sake let me go!

Truly the Greeks were wise who smiled,
    Saying, in days gone by,
Love has only the heart of a child
    And the wings of a butterfly!

(Ah, for the cabined sampans, floating free,
Ah, for the tropic moonlight nights, that fling
Unnecessary silver on a sea
Itself with phosphorescent light aglow.
Ah, for the waving palms along the shore.)

Craft, long laid up in a dockyard dry,
    Wearily yearn to feel
The cool caresses of living water
    Pressing against the keel.

A ship remembers the open sky
    Anchored in roadstead ease

And all that the wind and waves have taught her
   In far-off perilous seas.

Amidst the strife of clamorous speeches
   And eager gold-snatching hands,
The soul grows faint for the yellow beaches,
The loneliness of the wind-swept reaches,
   And the calm of Eastern lands.
My foot is athrill for the steel of the stirrup,
   My palms are astir for the grip of an oar
The whole of my body is sick for the sea
   And the peace of a desolate shore.

Perhaps you gave me what you call love,
   (I had called it another name)
Bunt anyway, I am tired of playing;
Take all the stakes of the sorry game.
I wonder you thought me worth betraying.
But what is there now that is worth the saying
   Since the end must be the same?

I shall piece together my broken youth,
   If aught of youth remain,
And when at last the wreck of me reaches,
Beyond the lilt of persuasive speeches,
   (I question if ever you spoke the truth)
The palm-tree shade of the coral beaches
The cool retreat of the Cinnamon grove,
   Peace will find me again.

For Youth, who sleeps so soundly and so well,
    On any couch and under any stars,
Shall join with Rest and weave a magic spell
    To soothe the memory of my prison bars.

Serenity shall raise pavilions o'er me,
    Freedom and dreams console me with a smile,
Hope, the Eternal Mirage, dance before me,
    And Love,—no more of love for me awhile!

I seek, to celebrate my glad release,
The Tents of Silence and the Camp of Peace.

That little island! surf-circled, it waits
    On the sapphirine waves for me,
To the right of the fairway through the Straits
    As you sail to the China Sea.

A pile built hut and a captive boat,
At the foot of the wavewashed stair afloat,
Blue water abreak upon the beach,
The soft, vague sound of Malayan speech,
Ah, the sun-gilt rest of that island shore,
Mine the folly to strive for more!

I shall go the way of the open sea,
    To the lands I knew before you came,
And the cool clean breezes shall blow from me
    The memory of your name.

The transient sorrow you cause me now
  Will fade away in the distance dim,
But Love is a God, and I wonder how
  You will make your peace with him!

The Consolation of Dreams

Farewell, O Sapphire Eyes, serene and clear,
    Tender and careless, not the stars above
Could take less heed of one who held them dear
    Than you, Beloved, who could not, would not, love.

Ah, Sapphire Eyes, who could not, would not, care
    Or shed on me their soft indifferent beams,
The long white day may keep you far as fair,
    Yet you come very near to me in dreams.

Dreams: when I force you with soft violence
    To turn on me their tender azure shine,
And tune your voice to this sweet eloquence
    "I am your lover, lend your lips to mine."

"Refuse me not." Ah, when would I refuse?
    "Turn here your face." When would I turn away?
I, whose one wish is that you should infuse
    Your life in mine in love's completest way.

I, who had held that life had given me all
    Had it, oh, if it had but given me you!
Had Fate but ordered your soft light to fall
    Across my solitudes, O eyes of blue.

In the Far East the old Religions say
   Man rises nearest to the Gods above,
For a brief space becoming even as they,
   In the last ecstasy of human love.

Might I not also rise and reach your soul
   If once its passionate life had passed to me
In the surrender of your self control,
   Th' unguarded moments of your ecstasy?

For though you hold that Love is brief and mortal,
   What other way can I attain to you?
I know, O Azure Eyes, no other portal
   To reach the mind beyond your mystic blue.

And yet—what use these dear, delusive dreams?
   The night wears through, the stars grow pale above,
Farewell, O Sapphires, set in tears, there seems
   No hope, no rest, you would not, could not, love.

Men Should Be Judged

Men should be judged, not by their tint of skin,
   The Gods they serve, the Vintage that they drink,
Nor by the way they fight, or love, or sin,
   But by the *quality of thought they think.*

The Island of Desolation: Song of Mahomed Akram

Here on the Island of my Desolation
    I look across the wastes of azure sea;
None of the ships that pass in exaltation
    Have any cargo or commands for me.

Not in the red of any joyous morning,
    Not in the gold of any sunset light,
Will they run up the flag to give me warning
    That the so longed-for vessel looms in sight.

Sometimes I light the beacon fires of passion
    To lure frail pleasure craft towards the shore,
Join the night revels in half-hearted fashion
    Only to wake more lonely than before.

Now and again some friendly soul has landed,
    Taken his careless welcome, sailed away;
And in the time of tempest, ships have stranded,
    Spilling rich merchandise about the bay.

White bones among the mangroves glisten dimly,
    Drift with the water, in the sunshine bleach,

While the gaunt ribs of wreckage rising grimly
    Guard the forlornness of the wind-swept beach.

Inland, among the fern and seeding grasses
    Where the Acacia, silken-tasselled, waves,
The summer wind sighs softly as it passes
    Over the green of half forgotten graves.

Little I heed; my eyes gaze ever seaward,
    Straining to glimpse the ship I never see,
My constant soul, set like a compass, theeward,
    Even as thine was always turned from me.

Ah, how I loved thee! Hoping to forget thee,
    Where are the things I did not vainly try?
But every cell and fibre still regret thee,
    Even in death remembrance will not die.

If thou shouldst seek me (though thou comest never,
    My hopes, like Lighthouse rays, stream forth to thee)
Thou wouldst still find me faithful, watching ever,
    Or buried with my face towards the sea.

A Sea Pink

She came, a maiden from the North,
   To dwell among a Southern race,
And lovely Northern eyes looked forth
   In azure from her oval face.

Her hair was like the pale faint gold
   September's sun sheds o'er the land,
And soft to touch and slim to hold
   The white perfection of her hand.

They loved her on that Southern shore:
   Tall fisher men and dark-haired boys
Were fain to linger round her door
   With shells and kindred ocean toys.

Yet was their love restrained by fear,
   So still she was, so calm and pale,
She seemed a star, remotely dear,
   No human love might dare assail.

Whilst in her chamber, small and bright
   With sea pinks and blue lavender,
She wondered through the summer night
   Why love had never come to her.

Her fancy wandered to the shore
   Sunburnt beneath the noonday skies,
Again the fisher lads she saw,
   Their willing arms and eager eyes.

Saw their young smiles, whose tender gleams
   Held all the love she had not known,
And, blushing in her morning dreams,
   Felt their red lips against her own.

But all day long her self-control
   Concealed her loneliness too well.
Alas! these barriers of the soul,
   So slight, yet so invincible!

Time passed: her azure eyes grew sad,
   Dull sorrow dimmed their dancing blue,
While many a pensive fisher lad
   Envied the seagulls as they flew.

Envied them their sweet liberty,
   Free of the ocean, free to love,
On light untrammelled wings, while he
   As well might woo the stars above

As the young maiden of his choice.
   Her gentle beauty bloomed in vain,
She knew no art, he found no voice
   To bridge the gulf between them twain.

How should a fisher lad aspire
  To win a thing as fair as this?
So after some days of dumb desire
  Some duskier maiden claimed his kiss.

And day by day the ripples broke
  Around the fishers in the bay.
Night after night alone she woke
  Till all her youth had passed away.

The swift sweet years when she was young,
  Her golden years, slipped lightly past,
And thus the song remained unsung,
  The rose ungathered till the last.

The Date-Garden

I dreamt last night you were mine indeed,
  And I prayed the dream to stay,
But this world of ours with reckless haste
  Rushed on to another day.

I thought we slept on the Desert sands,
  Where the old date-gardens lie,
And a golden mist of quivering stars
  Was scattered across the sky.

There, in the limitless silences,
  Where only the jackals live,
You were kind to me as you are not kind,
  And gave what you will not give.

And when the hands were fallen apart,
  And the longing lips grown loth,
A little wind from under the stars
  Came down and caressed us both.

Then, leaning against your heart, I said,
  Ah, it were a lovely thing
If from this blossoming time of ours
  Some flower of life should spring.

And though mankind, with its narrow sight,
  Might christen it child of shame,
The people's heart, which is always true,
  Would give it a sweeter name.

"Love-child": name that is tender with love;
  With joyous passion and youth.
Man's own sad laws have blinded his eyes,
  But some of us see the truth!

If mine own hand had written my fate,
  I know I had rather been
Fruit of a wild and exquisite love
  Than the child of dull routine.

Should I not give to children of yours
  Created in sheer delight,
The cool clear soul of this star-lit waste,
  The peace of the Desert night?

And all our fervour and youth and force,
  Would they not feel the same?
Surely the torch of life should be lit
  At the whitest heat of the flame!

Lean back, lean back, till your loosened hair
  Lies soft on the Desert sands,
That all yourself may abandoned be
  To my reverent lips and hands.

When first I saw you, My Well-Beloved,
    In my secret heart I said,
Ah, that the lips might follow the eyes
    And feast where these have fed!

And now that thine own have set mine free
    (Be still, O, my heart, be still)
I only fear that my life may wane
    Before they have had their will.

Thus I spoke in the visions of night,
    As I may not speak by day,
But the cruel hours with reckless speed
    Have carried my dream away.

The night is over, the stars have paled,
    The magic of sleep has flown,
The white-eyed Day, slipping into the world,
    Found me, as ever, alone.

Trees of Wharncliffe House

O<small>H</small>, green and leafy Wharncliffe trees
    That tremble to and fro,
You rustle in the languid breeze
    And catch the evening glow.
Across the dusty gloomy street,
    I note your tender sheen,
But unto me it is not sweet,
    Who see what I have seen.

The slender Coco palms I crave
    Beside the sea,
Where every phosphorescent wave
    Leaps up in ecstasy,
Towards the tangled stars above
    That sparkled in the blue,
These are the things I know and love.
    How can I care for you?

I always feel a sense of loss
    If, at the close of day,
I cannot see the Southern Cross
    Break through the gathered grey,

Nor watch the liquid moonlight gleam
    Among the temples white,
And realise that lovely dream,
    We call an Eastern night.

Though I, impatient of the heat,
    Forth from the window lean
To cool my sight across the street
    Amidst your shaded green,
Your leaves, refreshed by summer showers,
    Are naught to me, who feast
My fancy on those other flowers
    That burn about the East.

For I have seen the Lotus bloom
    On lakes like inland seas,
And white Magnolias, through the gloom,
    Moonlight among the trees.
Have watched the pale Tuberose, aglow
    With phosphorescent light,
And Water-lilies lying low
    On sacred tanks at night.

Have wandered where the Moghra flowers
    Exhale their scent at noon,
And dreamt sweet dreams where Jasmin bowers
    Grow white beneath the moon.
Have seen the Poppies' crimson wave
    O'erflow the land for miles

And Roses, on an Eastern grave
    Turn even Death to smiles.

By night, my fancy spreads her wings
    In visions that console,
But all day long, remembered things
    Are dragging at my soul.
I want the silver on the sea,
    The surf along the shore,
The ruined Mosque, whose weeds grow free,
    Where Princes prayed of yore.

I want the lonely, level sands
    Stretched out beneath the sun,
The sadness of the old, old lands,
    Whose destiny is done,
The glory and the grace, that cling
    About the mountain crest
Where tombs of many a faithless king
    Guard, faithfully, their rest.

Not lightly would I speak of Love,
    Or estimate his power,
But every star that wheels above,
    And each enamelled flower
That sends persuasive influence
    To touch the human mind,
Appeals to some strange, inner sense
    That Love can never find.

Love always needs his ally, Youth,
    Or lost is all his charm;
A sunset is a golden truth
    Nor age nor ill can harm.
And loveliness will lend the earth
    Its radiance and sheen
If but one rosebud come to birth,
    One single leaf grow green.

Ah, waving trees of Wharncliffe House,
    That tremble to and fro,
Old dreams and fancies you arouse,
    Old fires you set aglow.
Your shaded greenness soothes the eye,
    Worn out with dusty hours,
But still I crave that Eastern sky,
    Those brilliant Orient flowers!

All Farewells Should Be Gently Spoken

Ay, smooth your hair for another lover,
   Refold the satin, restring the pearls,
Lest those who will take my place discover
   Discoloured tints and dishevelled curls.

Lift up those delicate lips that mine
   Reddened with kisses but yesterday,
Let others drink the dregs of the wine
   We two have tasted and flung away.

I wish you well; go gather the gold,
   The little triumphs you hold so dear,
For you the pasture, the sheltered fold:
   Ways smoothed by custom and fenced by fear.

You could not have lived aloof, afar
   In golden deserts, by lonely streams,
Be rich, be courted, be all you are,
   But seek not silence, nor love nor dreams.

Yet what am I that my song should shame you,
   What strength have I, that I call you weak?

Ah, Love alone has the right to blame you
　　And He is a God and will not speak.

One thing there is yet to be glad of; Fate
　　In making us one has not left us three.
No child shall inherit our love's estate
　　To be false like you or forlorn like me.

What if your sweet and treacherous eyes
　　Had smiled at me from a child of mine,
Your delicate lips, so apt at lies,
　　Lived and laughed, a perpetual sign

Of fitful passion and frenzied hours
　　That now are utterly passed away,
Dead and forgotten as last year's flowers
　　And all sweet things that have had their day.

Yet, last farewells should be gently spoken,
　　And times of pleasure let no man grudge.
Of things once loved, though his heart be broken,
　　A lover has never the right to judge.

Garden Song

FORGIVE me, in that I kissed your lips
    Too fiercely or too soon;
It was the fault of the nightingale
    Singing against the moon.
If Reason swerved in a brief eclipse
    The while I sinned my sin,
Opposed to Love, it must always fail
    Since Love must always win.

The flowers rejoiced in that kiss of ours,
    Even as they were fain
The great night moths should ravage their hearts,
    Seeking for golden gain:
Bringing them pollen from other flowers,
    Set open through the night
To play their motionless, mystic parts
    In Nature's marriage rite.

And who was I, to resist, withstand
    That charm of fragrant gloom?
A summer night has a thousand powers
    Of scent and stars and bloom.

Forgive me, in that my errant hand
    Caressed your silken hair,
Oh lay the blame on the Orange flowers,
    You *know* how sweet they were!

The Match-Maker

MANY are loved, but few indeed adored
With the devotion paid to thee, O Lord.
She bids me steal the tassel of thy sword,
                            Thinking of love.

That she may fasten it above her bed,
Thus will some subtle sense of thee be shed,
When the wind blows across its gold and red.
                            Fancy of love!

Further, she bade me say these words to thee;
"Downcast and long although my lashes be,
Thine eyes have burnt into the heart of me."
                            Language of love!

"Mimosa wood, though on the threshold laid
And subject unto passing footsteps made,
Can still send forth fresh shootlets, unafraid."
                            Fable of love?

"Such is the tree's innate vitality.
And if my heart were trampled down by thee,

Still would new shoots of love arise from me!"
        Fervour of love!

As waits the sacrifice upon the pyre,
Fearing, yet longing for, the sacred fire,
Her beauty craves the flame of thy desire,
        Master of love.

There is an island in the Southern Sea,
Where maidens, when they children cease to be
With Festivals of Laughter are set free.
        Island of love.

Set free to love; none hinder them nor chide,
Laughing, they call their lovers to their side,
Laughing, their lovers leave them, satisfied,
        Joyous with love.

Go thou to her, such laughter will be thine.
And when her arms about thy youth entwine,
Thou wilt be grateful for these words of mine,
        Message of love.

I leave thee, Lord, and if thou shouldst consent,
And thus thy gracious life with hers be blent,
Remember in the days of thy content,
        This slave of love.

Vain-Glory

If you feel, in the Chaos of Things,
    Life is somewhat a sorrowful jest,
Come to the shadow of Love's soft wings,
    To starlight silence and dreams and rest.
Leaving the glory, the pomp, the power,
    Fame and fortune and folly and fret,
The Western sun is a golden flower!
    Come to love, come to forget!

Turn your tender and radiant eyes,
    Eyes like amethysts, jewelled and clear,
What do they see in the world to prize,
    Which of its baubles would they hold dear?
Vain are the glories, every one,
    Vain to conquer and vain to regret;—
The falling shadows engulf the sun,
    Come to love, come to forget!

The flag of Glory is quickly furled,
    The Sword of Honour is hardly more;
To those who wander about the world
    The standards vary; one is not sure.

One's drifting soul, in Life's ebb and flow,
   Would fain be faithful to some things yet,
But youth is calling, the sun is low,
   Come to love, come to forget!

From shade of sorrow or stress of strife,
   Here, in the desert, how far one seems.
Oh, follow your fancy, lend your life
   To the golden guidance of your dreams!
And come to me: you are free to go
   Ere ever the stars of morning set;—
The fires of sunset are burning low,
   Come to love, come to forget!

Worth While

I ASKED of my desolate shipwrecked soul,
    "Wouldst thou rather never have met
The one whom thou lovedst beyond control
    And whom thou adorest yet?"
Back from the senses, the heart, the brain,
    Came the answer swiftly thrown,
"What matter the price? We would pay it again,
    We have had, we have loved, we have known!"

Invitation to the Jungle

The Jungle gloom is dim and cool,
    And, even through the noonday heat,
Among the reeds beside the pool
    The silent air is freshly sweet.

Though desert winds, sand-laden, pass,
    And all the tree-tops bend and sigh,
No breezes stir the flower-filled grass
    Beside the lake where we shall lie.

We shall not hear the Temple bells,
    The tom-tom's sad insistent beat,
The far Bazaar, whose murmur swells
    With eager cries and restless feet.

We shall not know the myriad cares
    That make the Home's soft tyranny,
And all the Temple's lip-worn prayers,
    Its ordered gifts, will pass us by.

Those lip-worn prayers; whose sense is lost,
    Effaced by long and tearful use,

By thousands daily skywards tost,
   While still the Gods reject,—refuse,—

Let others pay the reverence due
   With waving lights and sacred flowers.
I pray no more except to you,
   My faith is in this love of ours.

And I shall twine the Kuskus grass
   To shield the thing I hold so dear.
What if the fierce-eyed Panthers pass?
   I know their ways and have no fear.

The jungle is my native land
   And love shall smooth its path for you:
Ah, could I make you understand,
   How well it is, this thing you do.

You leave the world, and passing by
   Its tarnished gold and futile strife,
Gain freedom, love, the open sky,
   The flowers upon the Tree of Life!

The Sinjib Tree

I AM the flowery Sinjib tree,
   The sweetest thing in the world,
With silvery leaves on a rugged stem
   And golden buds incurled.
Oh, traveller, turn thy face to me
   Ere ever thy tent be furled.

Bring here the maiden of thy desire
   In my scented shade to rest,
And be she cold as bitterest snow
   On Takht-i-Suliman's crest,
Yet she will open her arms to thee
   And entreat to be caressed.

And she shall crave for thy love and thee,
   Who was erst so coldly calm,
For the subtle scents of my honeyed flowers
   Shall soothe her like a charm,
Till she shall long for a child of thine
   To nestle within her arms.

For I am the Flower of Khorassan,
   The silvery Sinjib tree,

And he who pitches his camp beneath
  Shall dream of love and of me,
As my scented breath steals through the tent
  To enhance his ecstasy!

The Outlaw

Worn we lie on the shimmering sand,
  Well quit of the world and free.
The scent of the flowers that bloom inland
  Is wafted over the sea.

I lean on your shoulder, round and bare,
  As soft as a ripened peach,
And watch the weed, like a woman's hair,
  Drift up on the curving beach.

Twilight falls on the violet hills,—
  On silver turf at their feet,—
From groves of Orange a wild bird trills
  Songs that are cruelly sweet,—

Lilac and lemon and rose and grey
  Lie soft on the dimpled waves,—
The golden tribute of parting day
  Is laid on the Moorish graves.

The lonely dead, who are dispossessed:
  A Minaret marks their Creed,
Grim cactus hedges enshrine their rest,
  What need, my brothers, what need?

They faced the curses and cares of Life,
    And how should they fear in Death
The howls of the hoarse hyenas' strife,
    Their carrion tainted breath?

Nay, Well-beloved, why shudder and thrill
    When that graveyard meets your view?
Gardens or Rest, or Death if you will,
    Are closed for a while to you.

Safe in your youth, which is my reproach;
    I take it to stifle pain,
As men repel the waves that encroach
    From stress of the outer Main.

Building a dyke, or a strong sea-wall,
    But if this they fail to do,
Collecting wreckage, things slight and small,
    For these have their value too.

As massed together in heaps they lie
    Resisting the rising tide
And slowly, surely, the waves defy,—
    The builders are satisfied.

Thus have I taken your sixteen years
    To ward my sorrow away,
And your young eyes that have known no tears
    Look gaily over the bay

Towards the country of sober skies,
    The land of the sullen sea,
Where dwell the azure, disdainful eyes
    That never had light for me.

Many the rules in the stressful North!
    And wearier most than wise;
But though I wandered away, came forth
    From under those clouded skies.

Two laws are fixed, as the stars above,
    For every race and clime;
One is the cruel Sweetness of Love
    And one the Shortness of Time!

Ah, Well-beloved, though I may not spend
    The best of my soul on you,
Ask of me as you would of a friend,
    All that I can I will do.

For now that none have the right to say
    "This thing is not meet for thee,"
I take what happiness drifts my way
    Well quit of the world and free.

Return!

Serene and slender, and more than ivory white;
Whose Sphinx-like riddle it never was mine to read,
I implore Thee, by all our moments of past delight,
    Have pity! Take heed!

How long, O Lord, this crucifixion of me,
Whose whole soul faints for a word,—for a single touch?
Oh, Thou, whom I seek through Thy sinister mystery,
And, understanding so little, desire so much,
    Have pity on me!

Thy hair was gold, the pale, dim gold of the North,
Thy weary attitudes quiet in graceful rest,
But Thy tortured and desperate soul looked wildly forth,—
Through the eyes of a haunted man, distraught, distressed,
    By sorrow or wrath.

I would rather share Thy hell, that I dimly guess,
Than any alien heaven unknown of Thee.
Oh, out of Thine own despair, Beloved, heed my distress,
    And return to me!

Philosophy of Morning

SLAVE

"Ay, he is fair, yet not indeed so fair
  As thou transfigurest him
In thine own eyes, clear as the morning air.

"Ay, he is strong and lithe, yet not in truth
  As thou rememberest him,
'Tis the intoxication of thy youth!

"Mistress of mine, for once let truth be told,
  These lovers are less lovely than they seem,
'Tis love, how subtly turns their brass to gold
  With the alluring magic of a dream."

PRINCESS

"Thy chatter, girl, is like a nest of jays!
Disturb me not with jangling coffee trays!
Reclose the lattice and shut out the light,
I have no haste to end the peace of night.

(*Sings*) "He whom I love is like a lonely tower
         Lit by the sunlight of a great renown,

Aspiring skyward in unconscious power
   Above the dust and clamour of the town.

"The West wind fanned the battlemented crest,
   And, in the frolic of an idle hour,
Left a light seed among the stones to rest
   Which later bloomed a scented golden flower.

"Oh, Seomar, so much desired of me,
   Lovely and lone and lofty as thou art,
May it be written in my fate's decree
   To plant love's golden flower against thy heart!

"And if love be the dream thou say'st it is
What matter? so it bring that face of his
Near unto mine, and longing find relief.
I care not if the dream be true or no
So it be not too brief!"

Slave

" 'Tis ever so!
And still the young waste in Love's fitful flame
The force that else had brought them gold and fame."

Princess

"Didst thou not tell me of one who bought thy youth
   How that his age hindered his pleasure in thee?
Spite of his gold, gained without pity or ruth
   His uncut emeralds and pearls of the sea.

"And what of him who headed the tribes last year
   Against the Sultan? When he had lost the game,
Blinded and burnt, and broken with pain and fear,
   Cared he then for the passing Mirage of Fame?"

Slave

"Truly, men gain not much for all their strife!"

Princess

"There are some chapters in the book of life,
Pages whose print demands the morning light,
That youth alone can understand aright.
These I would read while time is with me still
Let after happenings be what they will.
For this I hold, that when a woman lies
Watching her beauty fire her lover's eyes
While the lithe strength she worshipped from afar,
Melts in her arms and quivers on her breast,
She knows the utmost sense of joy and rest
That fate has given to this luckless star
Men call the world.

   "And though the dream may fade,
Passing away, as sunshine into shade,
Memories of its light will still assuage
The weariness that haunts the after age.

"So shall she see the fire in other's eyes,
Hear the quick questions and the low replies,

And these shall not disturb her inward rest,
Since, in her spring she also knew the best.

"But those who let the days of youth drift by,
Scorning to share a lover's ecstasy,
They shall lament, when all their youth has flown,
Most bitterly, because they have not known.

"Ah, close the lattice, leave me to my dreams,
Shut out the brightness of the morning beams,
Let me return to night where silence is
And the worn beauty of that face of his."

The Slave

In purple haze the sun has set,
A tuft of palms, a Minaret,
    Rise clear against the sky.
The silence of the scented air
Stirs to a sense of evening prayer
    At the Muezzin's cry.

What care have I, that yesterday
I led thee as a slave away
    From Maroc's market-place?
Are we not all the slaves of love?
The very stars that wheel above
    Are bound by time and space!

I struck the fetters from thy hands
Only to forge thee stronger bands;
    Leastways, 'twas my desire
To hold thy captive soul to me,
Even as mine is chained to thee,
    By links of passionate fire.

I want thee for thy beauty's sake,
Though naught, as owner, will I take;
    Thou art entirely free.

Yet, if thy gaze of sombre fire
Find aught in me to wake desire
    Then give thyself to me!

The Seasons

YOUTH

Would God, that I could love thee less!
   My days are lost in dream of thee.
I do my work in weariness,
   Till kindly twilight sets me free.

Throughout the night thy beauty burns,
   The more possessed, the more desired.
Until another day returns
   To find me desperately tired.

MIDDLE AGE

Ah, me, that I could love thee more!
   I know thee kind; I see thee fair,
Why can I not, as oft of yore,
   In soft caresses lose my care?

At times life's dragging afternoon
   Is quickened by thy morning charms;
I seek thee, but alas! I soon
   Forget thee, even in thine arms!

Age

These lovers! Who can understand
   Their vivid joy, their wild despair?
He does but live to kiss her hand,
   And she would die to touch his hair!

Love is an enemy to Rest,
   Which surely is Life's dearest good,
Yet, something stirs within my breast
   And murmurs, "Once you understood!"

Devotion of Aziz to Mir Khan

Mir Khan

"And now, Aziz, I take my leave of thee."

Aziz

"Farewell, Mir Khan."

Mir Khan

"Hast thou no more to say?"

Aziz

"I, saying farewell to thee, take leave of all."

Mir Khan

"Thou knowest, Aziz, I shall return to thee. I do but leave thee now, at thy command."

Aziz

"Ay, at my prayer."

Mir Khan

"Indeed I shall return

Ere the fifth sunset gild these barren hills.
I would have stayed with thee; have stayed alone,
Did I not feel the truth of all thy words,
How that my name entails a greater risk
Than mine foster-brother, yet I go
Somewhat in doubt——"

Aziz

"I have no doubt at all,
Only go quickly, lest my heart should break!"

Mir Khan

"See, now, Aziz, it is but as thou sayest,
If I should stay, they will imprison me,
And hold me long, knowing my father's name
Makes me a hostage, worthy to be held,
Whilst thee they will not——"

Aziz

"Me they will not hold."

Mir Khan

"What dost thou murmur?"

Aziz

"Nothing. Go, Mir Khan.
The last faint light has left the lilac hills,

And thou shouldst start. Even disguised as now
In the disfiguring raiment of a slave,
Thy beauty shines like evening stars, ablaze
Through dusky mists that but enhance their glow.
Walk warily, Mir Khan, and hide thine eyes,
Lest women see, and passion shipwreck thee
Ere thou hast reached thy fort——"

Mir Khan

"Whence I return
With a picked squadron to deliver thee."

Aziz

"Why dost thou hesitate?"

Mir Khan

"Farewells are sad,
And—there is something in thine eyes, Aziz,
Dost thou?—thou canst not—doubt of my return?"

Aziz

"I doubt thee not, Mir Khan. Another star
Has risen above the purple mountain crest,
Thou shouldst be gone."

Mir Khan

"Believe me——"

Aziz

"I believe.
Indeed I know. Thine inmost secret thoughts
Are mine, were always mine. Ah, try me not,
Leave me, whilst I can bid thee leave me. Go,
Lest I implore thee, 'Stay and die with me!' "

Mir Khan

"Die? But thou diest not! I had not changed
My state and garments with thee, had a thought
Of death to thee, or even the chance of death,
Glanced on my mind. Nay, then, I stay, Aziz."

Aziz

"There is no risk. Thou art so much to me
Even a five days' parting moves me so,—
Breaks up my courage, till I hardly heed
What words I say. Go now. Thou art Aziz,
Aziz, the slave, remember, not Mir Khan,
Beloved of women, and ever in their snares,
Even as now."

Mir Khan
"Take thou my opium."

Aziz

"Nay, thou willst need it in the mountain pass;
I have my own."

Mir Khan

      "Thine own was given to me
Long since, thou knowest."

Aziz

         "I tell thee I want it not!"

Mir Khan

"Well, as thou willst, Aziz, farewell."

Aziz

           "Farewell."

  ·   ·   ·   ·   ·   ·   ·   ·

Aziz

"Ah, thou art gone indeed. Mir Khan, Mir Khan,
Return to me, return! I am lost! I am dead!
Is that the sound of his returning feet?
Nay, it is but a stone, his horse's hoof
Sets leaping down the hillside. Oh, Mir Khan,
Thou art gone from me, and my life is gone with thee!

"Ay, thou hast gone, and left me to my fate.
Knowing I knew thou knewest. For thou didst know.
Last midnight, when Sher Afzul came to me
And told me the Shah-Zada had decreed
That thou shouldst die, for that light love of thine

Amongst his women, also he made known
Thou hadst arranged to change with me, to say
'Stay thou, Aziz, while I, Mir Khan, return
To bring thee speedy succour from the fort.
And if they find that thou art but Aziz,
Aziz, the slave, and not the lord Mir Khan,
They will not wrong thee, will not torture thee
As they would torture me, the son of kings.'

"Further, Sher Afzul said thou, smiling, spak'st
Saying, 'He loves me so, he will remain,
Even with certain death confronting him.'

"Ay, but thou knew'st me well. He *will* remain!
There was no need of any speech of thine
To bid me stay. Am I not thine indeed
For life or death? Oh, I am glad, Mir Khan!
Glad that thou givest me this exquisite gift,
Even the gift of death,—death for thy sake.

"Thy beauty was ever a perfect thing to me,
Gracious and free; to see thy luminous eyes
Lit with the longing of thine ardent soul,
Ablaze, like golden suns, in love or war,
To touch thy feet, setting thy stirrup-irons,
Or rest my lips upon thy drinking-cup,
These were the joys of Aziz, serving thee,
Living unnoticed with thee, in the tents.

"Women have loved me, even me, Mir Khan,
Not with the adoration given to thee,
But with kind words, and gentle ways, that fell
On my worn heart as rain on dusty flowers,—
Perhaps it was pity, not love; I do not know.
But this devotion that I have for thee,
This is another thing; I have no words
To tell thee what thou knewest and didst not heed.
Why shouldst thou heed? What could I do for thee,
To whom the whole world is willing to give its all,
Holding that all less than the sight of thee?

"When at to-morrow's dawn they torture me,
Burning my eyes, I shall remember thine,
The luminous circles of light I so adored.
And when they crush my limbs, I shall find peace
Knowing that thine, safe in the distant fort,
Amongst thy household rest in licit love.

"How I have envied them the things they did!
The women who loved thee, and were loved by thee.
Envied their jewelled hands the right to play
In that soft hair of thine, their little teeth
The law they allowed themselves to cling and bite
Thy rounded shoulder, I, who was naught to thee,
Set to prepare the couch, to smooth the quilt——

"Once I remember, crouched against thy tent,
I sought for warmth (thou wouldst have pardoned me

So cold it was that night) and heard her speak,—
Her, who beside thee, tranced in pleasure lay,
Saying, 'It is not for thy beauty's sake
That I desire thee so, but for thy fame,
Sweeping aside thine enemies, as leaves
Are blown by autumn gusts,' and thy reply
Was, 'Ah, Delight, art thou so sure of this?
Wouldst thou have sought and loved me had I been
Ill-favoured, say, as my poor slave, Aziz?'

"Ah, poor indeed! I heard nor cared no more,
Shivering in my furs upon the snow,
Not from the cold, but from the icy pangs
Of pain that will be with me till I die.
Truly, to-morrow's torments will not be
Crueller than these memories of mine.
The heated irons, the flesh-dividing steel,
Are they not gifts from thee, my well-beloved?

"Ah, when they lead me out, beyond the walls,
I shall look forth, across the rosy hills
Knowing that far beyond their lilac rims
Thou wilt awake, in all thy beauty's pride,
Safe and beloved, already forgetful of me,
Whose lonely and smouldering life has broken at last
Into this passionate flame of death. Mir—Khan——"

The Purple Dusk

Since the white day must dawn again so soon,
   And early love is diffident and shy,
Oh, charitable clouds, conceal the moon,
   Grant the indulgence of an unstarred sky!

Ah, silver surf, abreak along the shore,
   Cease for a while thy restless ebb and flow.
The silence trembles with thy sullen roar
   And the soft voice I love is very low.

Wind of the Desert, leave the Orange flowers
   To spill their sweetness over sand and sea,
Come, all unperfumed, to this couch of ours;
   Blow through his curls and bring their scent to me.

Ah, Time, who brought this treasure to my breast,
   Knowing so well that cruelty of thine,
I would die now, and leave thee at thy best,
   Ere thou hast torn my lover's lips from mine.

Hamlili, the Sultan of Song

ALAS, for the fate of Hamlili,
The slender fanatical singer,
Whose fingers were skilled on the ginbri;
    Who played the tears into men's eyes.
Who harped on men's hearts till they quivered
And swayed on the border of madness,
Vibrating and twisting in passion:
    Hamlili: the Singer of Sighs:

Hamlili: Beloved in the Soko:
Whose song was as rest to the weary.
As Lips of the Loved to the Lover.
    Hamlili: Assuager of Care.
Whose tears clustered thick on his lashes.
As, torn from the heart of the ginbri,
The music, caressive and tender,
    Arose in the tremulous air.

They took him, the victim of slander,
And burnt out his eyes in the Kasbah,
They cut off the hand of Hamlili,
    The hand that was Lord of the Strings,

Whose slender and delicate fingers,
Persuaded the lute as a lover
Persuadeth the heart of his mistress
    To tender and passionate things.

Ah, none will now pause in the Market,
To hear in the twilight of springtime,
When flowers that bloom in the country,
    Have scented the heart of the town,
The songs of that Sultan of Singers,
We called the Caresser of Lutestrings,
Who lies in the gloom of the Kasbah,
    Whose lute is for ever laid down.

Love Is the Symbol of a Sacred Thing

*W*HO scans the pedigree, nor shrinks to trace
   Some link unlawful? Yet he had not been
Had this illicit love not taken place,
   Or that forbidden face remained unseen.

They who say *any* love is coarse or light,—
   Even the brief caresses of an hour,
The careless kisses of a summer night,—
   Condemn the root, not knowing of the flower.

When graceless actions of some casual twain
   Seem but the surge of Youth, the heat of Wine,
His search for Pleasure, or her hope of Gain,
   May be the vassals of some vast design.

For who can tell what life may come to birth,
   Prophet or Captain of the time to be
As from light seed, flung on the careless Earth
   Breaks forth a flower, that scented mystery.

And though from an embrace no fruit may spring
   Or from a kiss no spark be kindled, still

Love is the Symbol of a Sacred Thing

Love is the Symbol of a sacred thing,
   Through which the Unseen Powers work their Will.

Those unknown Gods, who move behind a veil
   No mortal sense may ever hope to lift;
We only know they falter not nor fail,
   And they have granted us one lovely gift.

This Gift of Love, which we condemn, despise,
   Bending it to the baseness of our will.
Yet in the lowest depths that passion lies
   It surely keeps some heaven-born fragrance still.

Therefore, O you, who find the Perfect Way,
   Scorn not the lesser, lighter loves you see,
Unworthy though they seem, yet who shall say
   Fate works not through them, for the Days to Be?

Istar-i-Sahara

Dim in the east the ruined city lies,
Purple, against the paler purple skies,
And slender palms and minarets arise
        Into the night.

The sands are soft; by desert winds caressed
Into a thousand ripples. Let us rest
And watch the flaming scarlet of the west
        Fade into night.

The pale pink Persian rose is like my mouth,
Thy breath is sweet as breezes from the south
To weary lands repining in the drouth
        Long days and nights.

I too have waited, parched and worn with pain,
Come and refresh me, as the gracious rain
Falls on tired fields and makes them green again
        Through summer nights.

Ah, how I love thee. Thou art very fair,
Witness the silken softness of thy hair,

And thy calm eyes, clear as the morning air
          On mountain heights.

Gloom falls apace, and silence spreads afar,
Give me thy hands, how slim and cool they are.
Lives there such love on any other star
          That shines to-night?

Ah, wait awhile, as yet I only care
To lie to leeward and drink in the air
That passes over thee and through thy hair,
          Bringing delight.

Withdraw thy lips from mine, Insatiate!
Ah, give me time, Beloved—thou willst not wait?
Then,—as thou willst, how shall I strive with fate
          This night of nights?

Star of the Desert, make me thine indeed,
Though thou shouldst slay me now, I should not heed.
Of future days and nights I have no need
          After this night.

My lips live only when they cling to thine,
Part them a little as they close on mine,
So I may crush the grape and drink the wine
          Of my delight.

If thou hast hurt me? Ah, how should I know?
If this be pain, then always pain me so!
Nay, do not stir, I cannot let thee go
        This night of nights!

Justly I worship thee! Thou art divine,
Creating thus thy life anew in mine.
Istar-Sahar! give me a child of thine
        This night of nights!

Love the Careless

Death one knows, and can meet, and torture and war,
All the varied horrible things of life.

But a lover is so defenceless. He cannot return
An open stab from the one beloved, or a secret thrust,
He has laid down his arms, and can but accept the words
                                                that burn
Into the depth of his soul. What can I do?
Though you shatter trust
And sin in every way that man can sin against Love.
I cannot enter the strife,
Cannot even implore,
Upbraid, reprove,
For I loved, and thrice cursed fool that I am! I love you
                                                  still.
All that I had of passion, of power, even of life,
Was laid at your feet. It did not avail me aught.

Does it ever avail?
All that was ever given or done or dared
If the one beloved be unwilling, can only fail.
Yet I know the value of what I have given—of Love.

The silver and gold of the Earth are no bribes for Him,
Nor will He stoop to a lure.
Kings have knelt, imploring, and only heard
On the lips they loved and longed for, reiterate "Nay,"
And the eyes of Beauty itself, perfect and pure
Have wasted useless tears; grown faded and dim,
And Love the Careless has not cast them a thought.

Still, if you wish to throw love away, throw it away!
If you desire to squander my gifts, do as you will
With values you never comprehended or even knew.

Once I saw the Summer of Love in your eyes,
Therefore to-day my hands are no longer free;
I am dumb as the silent skies.

A lover is so defenceless. I only pray
That Fate in the future deal gentlier, Beloved, with you
Than you ever have dealt with me!

Should Thou Consent

Thou knowest, Lord, that my desire
   Is to be thine indeed;
Though thou, alas, of love or me
   Hast neither note nor need.

Ah, though thou canst not give thyself
   My longing to allay,
Yet grant me some small privilege
   To take my pain away.

If once thy lips were laid on mine
   (Canst thou not spare me this?)
I could enchant myself in dreams
   With memories of thy kiss.

What is a small caress to thee?
   Given,—forgotten quite,—
But unto me, shouldst thou consent,
   An infinite delight!

The Gods who send the sacred flame
   Upon the altar pyre

Remain afar, serenely calm
  Untroubled by desire.

But the glad worshipper below
  Falls faint in ecstasy;—
Thus would it be, shouldst thou consent,
  Between thyself and me!

Reminiscence of Maeterlinck's "Life of the Bee"

Oh, for the death of a beautiful purple bee,
    Sailing away to the blue of a limpid sky;
To have yielded up one's life in an ecstasy,
    And then, in the very climax of love, to die!

To give oneself completely, once and for ever;
    Drink life at its utmost height as one laid it down;
Spend one's soul in the rush of one last endeavour;
    And rule supremely in laying aside the crown.

On Deck

Truly the couch is hard to outward seeming,
    The vessel sways on the unquiet sea,
Yet what care I? who nightly in my dreaming
    Lay your soft hair between the planks and me.

Storms have delayed us, and the cargo, shifted,
    Lists us to leeward as the breakers roll,
I had not cared, not even though we drifted
    Out to uncharted oceans round the Pole.

There was a Rani once, who long neglected,
    Nightly arrayed herself in silk and gold,
Waiting the footsteps, loved and long expected—
    Waiting the lover, whom she could not hold.

Once on her wedding night, indeed, he sought her,
    Once, and once only; then his ardour died.
All sequent evenings of her youth but brought her
    A great desire ever unsatisfied.

Nightly she lay, her tears and jewels gleaming
    In the dim silver from the stars above,

Nightly her limbs, unconscious in her dreaming,
   Still took the tender attitudes of love.

For twenty years hope lingered, unabated,
   Though beauty lost its bloom and youth its fire,
Never there came the step for which she waited,
   Never the lover of her heart's desire.

Yet who shall weigh what subtle consolation
   Solaced the Rani in her lonely sleep;
When her locked arms in love's divine elation
   Held him whom, waking, she had failed to keep.

Thus I, who watched the alien planets gleaming
   Over the waters of this restless sea,
Drift back to sleep, and ever in my dreaming
   Lay your soft hair between the deck and me.

The Ocean Tramp

Where have you been, O wandering soul?
   I have journeyed far and wide;
I drift to a home in any port
   Drift out upon any tide.

And what have you lost, O restless soul?
   I have left, it seemeth me,
A bit of my youth in all the ports
   That are clustered round the sea.

What have you learned? The stress of the shore,
   The deep sea's desperate strife,
Some secret knowledge of men and things
   And the undertow of life.

Found you no happiness anywhere
   In the countries where you roved?
Once, only once,—a handful of nights,—
   With one whom I met and loved.

The Mirrored Stars of Tangier

It was the darkest hour before the dawn,
The orange-scented air was strangely sweet
And stars flashed brilliantly beneath our feet,
Reflected in the level sands, that lay
Lonely and mirror-like, around the Bay.

Lightly we walked on those reflected stars,
Gleaming among the drift and tangled spars
Left by the waves upon that lucent lawn
Whose flowers were planets.

                Then ourselves we flung
Down on the soft, wet sand, and all the skies,
Where countless, jewelled constellations hung,
Lay near and lovely to our wistful eyes.

Upon one silver star my lips were passed;
A vivid gem, than shone in Cassiopea,
No longer far away, and unpossessed,
But close beneath me, tremulously clear.

And I, who love a thing remote and far,
Drew courage from that sand-encircled star.
For, as my lips caressed its silver fire,
So might my arms embrace my Heart's Desire.

At Simrole Tank

"May you be tortured living, burned when dead,
  Your camels die, and virtue leave your wife!"
But he, who sat beneath the Peepul, said,
  "Why wish him more than average human life?"

The Guru's Tale:
The Enchanted Night

WHEN falling evening cooled the air,
   The Guru, in the twilight dim,
Caressed his Chela's silken hair
   And told this tale of love to him.

"Once, on the march to Bikanir,
   I, halting by a wayside well,
Beheld a woman drawing near
   Who cast on me a magic spell.

"Not hers the beauty, day by day
   Soliciting by tender lures,
But that which strikes the heart straightway,
   And instant victory ensures.

"She murmured, stretching forth her arms,
   Her red, love-thirsty lips apart,
'At sunset,—under yonder palms,—
   Come to my garden,—and my heart!'

"Ah, that unending afternoon!
  The sun seemed tethered in the sky.
I felt my inmost senses swoon
  With my desire's intensity.

"The silver twilight came at length,
  I reached the garden cool and sweet,
And all my eager youth and strength
  Lay at her small and jewelled feet.

"Three nights we gathered our delight:
  I had almost kissed her lips away,
Yet still her eyes, alert and bright,
  Resented the invading day.

"Alas, the fourth delirious eve
  Ended in terrified surprise:
Her lamp alight she was wont to leave
  For love allured her through the eyes.

"This night she cried in passionate pain,
  Her heart seemed broken in her breast,
'Thy beauty is too great a strain,
  Let us put out the light and rest.'

("Perchance you hold the speech too strong,
  Or my recording it, conceit,

Ah, surely one who has lived so long
    May own her words were true as sweet.)

"Then I, half rising to obey,
    Beheld a strange and terrible sight,
'Take not,' she said, 'thyself away,
    For I will quench the offending light.'

"She raised her arm, bejewelled and small,
    It lengthened,—stretched across the room,—
Put out the light on the opposite wall,
    And then,—diminished in the gloom!

"My pulses stopped, my passion died;
    The square, rose-scented chamber ran
To thrice our length, from side to side,
    And yet her arm had bridged the span!

"I wrenched myself from her embrace,
    And, heeding not her desperate cry,
Fled from that strange, enchanted place
    As deer before the Cheetah fly.

"Beneath the starlight, cool and clear,
    I raced across the sands alone,
And realized in stricken fear
    No mortal mistress I had known.

"My spirit told me, as I sped,
   Some tortured soul, escaped from hell,
One of the lonely, loveless dead
   Had risen and wooed me by the well.

"Ah, Best-Beloved, though Youth be sweet,
   He leads us to strange depths and heights.
Now leave me; later we shall meet
   For worship with the Circling Lights."

Among the Fuchsias

CALL me not to a secret place
    When daylight dies away,
Tempt me not with thine eager face
    And words thou shouldst not say.
Entice me not with a child of thine,
    Ah, God, if such might be,
For surely a man is half divine
Who adds another link to the line
    Whose last link none may see.

Call me not to the Lotus lake
    That drooping fuchsias hide,
What if my latent youth awake
    And will not be denied?
Ah, tempt me not for I am not strong
    (Thy mouth is a budded kiss)
My days are empty, my nights are long.
Ah, why is a thing so sweet so wrong
    As thy temptation is?

At the Taking of the Fort

"INAYET KAHN, I have no love for thee!"
  "When have I asked for love? Lie still and learn
Beneath the stars, how I would give thee all."
  "But thou art hurting me, thy kisses burn!"

"I shall not hurt thee, if thou willst consent,
  Resist me not, thou dost but fire my brain,
Hinder thou canst not; see, I loose thy hands
  And in a moment capture them again."

"Ah, thou art cruel!" "I shall be crueller yet!
  Wherefore refuse? I am thy destiny.
Millions of years lie ever we were born
  It was decreed that I should come to thee.

"Accepting me thou dost accept thy fate,
  Since it is written man was born to slay,
Slay and be slain, and women in their turn
  Renew the wasted lives that fall away.

"Ah, blame me not, it was not I who made
  This sad chaotic world that wounds us so

With life and love and death,—aimless alike——"
  "Inayet Kahn! have pity, let me go!"

"For this I slew; for this, I took the fort,—
  Crashed through the horrors of the blood-stained fight,
To the cool twilight and thy chill dissent——"
  "Never will I be slave to thy delight."

"This knife may mar a beauty that resists,
  And spoil my pleasure." "Slay, then, and have done,
Thus there will be no pleasure. Safe in death
  I shall escape from thee, oh, pitiless one!"

"Nay, for thy slender frame would keep its warmth
  Quite long enough for me to slake this thirst,
This dear and desperate need I have of thee;
  Ah, the desire thou couldst have curbed at first,

"In thy resisting arms has grown so great
  I needs must have thy beauty for my own.
Though Destiny decrees that I repel
  The only lovely thing my life has known!

"I have lived hardly all my days, God knows;
  Little of women's love has come my way;
Strive not with me, thou dost but make me cruel;
  I could be tender if thou wouldst obey.

"Ay, with a tenderness beyond all words
  Could shed my very soul beneath thy feet,
Lay down the whole of youth for one short hour,
  If thou wouldst share that hour and find it sweet.

"I had such dreams about this night with thee:
  All through the fight I saw these planets shine.
With each new wound my desperate spirit sobbed
  Let me but live to reach this roof of thine!

"And I *have* reached it; cool the night-wind blows
  Against these lips, whose fevered prayers are vain.
My broken ankle, dragging on the stone,
  Has pained me not as thy repulses pain.

"Ah, my beloved one; try to understand;
  Pity this burnt-up mouth with one cool kiss,
Thus shalt thou make my madness slave to thee,—
  Aie! then thou wouldst escape? take this and this!!

· · · · · · · ·

"So it is dead; the little and lovely thing,
  Pinned by my dagger to the earthen floor
Like a wired flower. Ah, well, I had my way,
  The small clenched hands resisted me no more.

"The soft curved lips spoke no repelling words,
  I can die now for I am satisfied,

And after death I shall demand no more
   Since I have had my heaven before I died.

"Now for my knife; thou life-long friend of me,
   Reluctantly thou leav'st her breast for mine;
Well,—'tis the sweetest blood that thou hast drawn
   Who hast drawn much; I did my work, do thine——"

Twilight

Come to me with the earliest star,
    Thou shalt not be caressed,
For passion and love shall stand afar
    That I may give thee rest.
Tell of thy troubles before we sleep
    Of all thy hopes and fears,
And if the telling should make thee weep
    Then I will drink thy tears.

The shade shall solace thy soul that grieves,
    And I shall shield thine eyes,
With glossy fans of magnolia leaves,
    From starlight in the skies,
While all the cares of the angry hosts
    That stalk thy soul by day
Between the trees, like wandering ghosts,
    Shall softly steal away.

Where shouldst thou slumber, if not with me?
    Thy haven is my breast,
I stretch myself as a couch for thee,
    To lull thy limbs to rest.

But, oh, I promise, Lover of mine,
  By all the stars above
I will not offer my lips to thine,
  Nor weary thee with love!

To Aziz

Ay, thou art fair; I know that beauty well.
Have I not longed for it as those in Hell
      Long for release?

Thou wouldst be kind to me? but when I craved
Such kindness in the days it could have saved
      Thou didst not cease

To torture me, Aziz, and now that Fate
Has brought me what so long, I so desired,
      It is too late,
      I am too tired.

In the Vineyards

LIGHTLY I valued my youth, as a trivial bloom,
   Shared with the rose in the hedgerows, the peach on the tree,
Till his lips had fallen fiercely on mine in the gloom
   Saying they found youth sweet; then it grew dearer to me.

Ah, my light-hearted youth, that I knew not aright!
   (Softly insistent he spoke through the heat of the day)
This, in the vine-hidden heart of a midsummer night,
   Was resigned in his forceful arms for ever and aye.

In the African Desert

Ah, but his lightest kiss was more sweet to me
Than any caress of thine, O silver sea!
His arms have held me gentlier e'en than thou,
In thy liquid, green embraces, hold'st me now.

Soft and cool as his breast, is thy foam above,
Even as soft as his ways and swords of love.
Yet was his cruelty as the jagged teeth
Of the hungry, lurking rocks that lie beneath.

Over the reef thy ripples are breaking now,
Curled, as the soft, dark clusters around his brow.
Grim as an octopus in its darkened lair,
Ghastly and sinister thoughts lay hidden there.

Pale he was and quiet, with reticent eyes,
Sombre and flecked with gold as the midnight skies.
They whispered the savage blood of desert kings
Ran in his veins and stung him to cruel things.

Maybe; I know not,—care not—against his breast
I found a secret garden of joy and rest.

Yet his desire, though fierce, was a fleeting breath
And mine, alas, is a flame that burns till death.

"Here in my tent is a couch prepared for thee,
Rest thou awhile and slumber, awaiting me."
Kindly he spoke, when the weary march was done
And the camp-smoke rose across the setting sun.

Down I lay in the shadow; I did not see
That cactus thorns were the couch prepared for me.
Ah, the pain of that feverish, endless night,
And the fainting sleep that came with morning light.

Waking I found myself on the soft warm sands,
While he withdrew the thorns with remorseful hands,
Saying, "Forgive me again, and thou shalt rest
To-night, as thou desirest, against my breast."

Strange and sweet were the ways where his fancy trod,
A panther's fierceness linked to dreams of a God,
Passion, wild as the Desert, in strength and power,
Lips as soft and fresh as the touch of a flower.

These were his gifts of atonement through the night.
These, with persuasive words that enhanced delight,
And strange, sad songs and legends, which left his eyes
Aglow with the fire of sombre memories.

One still night, on the breast of a starry sea,
"Row, till I bid thee cease," he ordered me.
The skin wore through, and the paddle ends were red,
Before, when the sunrise came, the word was said.

Yet as the starlight fell on his long, lithe grace,
The vivid and tender beauty of his face,
I could have prayed that the night should never cease
And cursed the rosy morning that brought release.

Over the rocks he would swing me, to and fro,
Where the white surf foamed a thousand feet below,
Would smile and murmur, "I will not loose thee—quite,
This graceless body of mine needs thine to-night."

Locked in his hut, through the ardent heats of June,
He would not allay my thirst, by night or noon,
Saying, "If water and wine be held from thee
More eagerly willst thou drink my lips and me."

He pinned my lower lip to the lip above,
"Lest thou in my absence utter words of love."
With pointed shells he pricked on my breast his name,
"That thou may'st keep the stamp of thy love and shame."

What cared I? In the joy of passion's blindness
Little I recked of kindness or unkindness.

Only now, when he leaves me in lonely peace,
My torment begins because his tortures cease.

Never will any freshness of thine, O sea,
Allay this endless fever alight in me.
He could assuage with his cruel, tender hands,
But alas, he neither heeds nor understands.

The City: Song of Mahomed Akram

Sinning, and sinned against, the City lay,
Burnt by the sun's caresses day by day,
Passive, defenceless, with her latest breath
Conceiving at his pleasure plague and death.

Relentlessly he poured his ardent rays
Into her cloistered courts and secret ways,
While the hot gold he spilt upon the plain
Rose from the furnace of the sands again.

Beneath a sullen sunset, dimly red,
Rent by the lamentations for the dead,
Whose burning-ghats defiled the stagnant air,
The breathless city waited in despair.

Then came the flutter of a sudden breeze,
Fragrant with scents of aromatic trees,
Cool with the magic freshness of the sea,
And the dry maize-leaves shivered restlessly.

The wind went onwards, to the outer gate,
Thrilled with soft pity for the City's fate,

Dispensing coolness, passed the inner wall,
And fanned the lips of those about to fall.

Swept in his freshness through the stifling lane,
Flew through low casements, fluttered forth again,
Winnowed the market-place whose floor was red,
And lightly smoothed the cereclothes of the dead.

Stole through the women's chambers, close and sweet,
Lifted their clinging silks from face to feet,
Cooled the pale brows that glimmered in the dusk,
Then gained the open faintly tinged with musk.

Entered the prison, soothed the ring-worn wrist,
The deeper wounds of fettered ankles kissed,
Giving the only freedom that was craved;
Freedom from heat. Thus was the City saved.

His coolness left her fresh as any flower,
And to restrict the sun's relentless power,
He veiled her with soft clouds and bid them stay
Till all the heat-wrought ill should pass away.

I would have asked such aid of thee, had I but dared,
Thou couldst have done as much for me, hadst thou but
cared.

The Jungle Fear

When sunset lights are burning low,
While tents are pitched and camp-fires glow,
Steals o'er us, ere the stars appear,
The furtive sense of Jungle Fear.

For when the dusk is falling fast
Still, as throughout the Ages past,
The stealthy beasts of prey arise
And prowl around with hungry eyes.

Though safe beside the fire I sit
And stretch contented hands to it,
Though all the cheerful camping-ground,
With men and arms, is close around,

I feel the Jungle very near
And shiver with instinctive fear.
For in some hidden cells of me
Stirs the ancestral memory

Of times when from the beasts of prey
At this same hour men slunk away

To seek their caves, and thrilled to hear
The red-eyed Panthers lurking near,

Or the weird, melancholy howl
Of famished packs of Wolves a-prowl.
Long centuries have since passed by
But still these instincts will not die.

And even men in Cities pent,
Who never slept beneath a tent,
Have said that they at twilight feel
The same strange fear across them steal.

Hid in our being, dim and deep,
The terrors of past perils sleep,
A heritage obscure and vast
From Man's unfathomable past.

Each twilight, when the sun burns down
In desert waste, or crowded town,
When shadows fall and night draws near
The dusk brings back the Jungle Fear.

Disloyal

You were more than a Lover to me,—
  Were something sacred, and half divine,—
Akin to Sunset over the Sea,
  To leaves that tremble and stars that shine.

There was not much to attract in me,
  No gift or beauty; you did not care
Enough to give me fidelity
  Who cared so deeply, and could not share.

Alas, my Temple! I find the Shrine
  I entered barefoot, with bended head,
To pay that tender homage of mine,
  An open courtyard, where all may tread!

And all men knew it, I hear, but I,
  Who being a trusting fool, it seems,
Went to the Market of Love to buy
  With coins of worship, and faith, and dreams!

Still it is over. Now, to forget!
  I know not whether to choose anew

In hopes of finding loyalty yet,
    Or, fond but faithless, drift on with you.

Loving you lightly, among the rest,—
    (Many a little, not greatly one),—
You may be right: I may find it best
    To do, henceforward, as you have done.

But ah, for my sweet, lost nights with you,
    When had Death been, in the dawning grey,
Price of your beauty and love, I knew
    I would have paid, and been glad to pay!

The Court of Pomegranates

The Rani, decked in silk and pearls,
With Jasmine flowers among her curls,
Said, while the stars grew bright above,
"Draw near, O girls, and speak of love!"

JAI (*the fan-weaver*)

"Ah, how shall I tell thee of love, O Queen,
   For mine was knotted with hate;
With a dancing-girl he had faithless been
   And rendered me desolate.

"He lay in the Tamarind shade at rest,
   Where Hunuman's Temple is,
And a little knife crept out of my breast
   To bury itself in his!"

TINCHAURYA (*the scent-sprinkler*)

"If Fate should say, 'Thy course is run,'
   It would not make me sad;
All that I wish to do is done,
   All that I would have, had.

My Lord has left his life with me,
    And mine divinely glad!

"They tell me I may be deceived,
    I neither care nor know,
A lesser love might well be grieved,
    With me it is not so.
My Lord has lain within these arms,
    And all the rest may go!"

One of the Deva-dasi
(girls dedicated to a Temple)

"Shrivelled and aged, with never a rest,
I wearily wander from Shrine to Shrine.
But Vishnu is branded across my breast;
The Gods themselves were once lovers of mine!"

Lala *(the door-keeper)*

"I went to him as a willing bride,
    He did not use me ill,
A little, perhaps, he broke my pride
    Against his reckless will.

"But any sorrowful time of tears
    Through which he made me go,
I minded not, for in after years,
    I loved his children so!"

Yasmini (*the dancing-girl*)

"I am clothed with the gold and the kisses of men
    And, nightly, new love-songs impassion the air;
For a while I shall dance in the torchlight, and then
    Comes darkness; and desolate depths of despair.

"Oh, Daughters of Virtue, to you it is given
    To lull with caresses new life at the breast;
By us, in our beauty, unshamed though unshriven,
    The Youth of the Nation is firstly possessed."

Gulabi (*a slave*)

"The thing we love has endless charms
    To while away our discontent;
Men seldom feel the weight of arms,
    Or women that of ornament.

"Her hair is softer far than mine,
    Her gold-starred teeth more almond white,
Her eyes so often mirror thine,
    Small wonder they are always bright!

"Her happiness unmoved I see,
    Though I am naught and she is wed,
Because the child thou gavest me
    Is living still, and hers is dead!"

The Rani

"How like we are, how all the same,
We think one thought, we play one game,
        Beneath one sceptre bend.
To careless slaves or curtained queens
Love is our most delightful means
        To a delightful end."

The Tower of Victory

The starlight night was cool and dim,
    Soft clouds beflecked the tranquil sky.
She climbed the hill, and reached with him,
    The carven Tower of Victory.

The Tower that rears its lonely head
    Above the Jungle, wild and vast,
And dreams, perchance, of warriors dead
    Who held the hills in ages past.

Sweet fragrance drifted o'er the land
    From Champa trees and Jasmine flowers;
The lovers wandered, hand in hand,
    Through long, and all uncounted, hours.

And when the night was mid-way spent
    They climbed the dark and broken stair,
Half stifled from the acrid scent
    Of countless bats, that harboured there.

The topmost steps had fall'n away,
    A time-worn ladder took their place,

Until she felt the night-wind play
    In coolness on her upturned face.

At last, they reached the highest stage,
    Wind swept and open to the stars.
The battlements were worn with age
    But waving grasses hid the scars.

The lonely Jungle lay serene,
    Beneath the star-bejewelled skies,
They turned them from the silver scene
    To seek once more each other's eyes.

But when he caught her to his breast
    She shrank in delicate dismay;
So, chilled, he left her uncaressed
    And drew his eager arms away.

Her eyes beneath their lashes hid
    The tender tears that left them dim,
As down the ladder-rungs he slid
    And drew it swiftly after him.

"It must," he cried, "be naught or all;
    And I shall come no more to thee
Till from the Tower I hear thee call
    To say thou wilt be kind to me!"

"Stay *now*," she begged. He would not heed,
    But down the ruined, twisting stair

He crushed his way with reckless speed
    And reached the scented outer air.

But when he scarce had left the Tower
    He paused, and felt his anger cease,
Such was the magic of the hour,
    Its lovely mystery and peace.

. . . . .

Two eyes among the thickets glow;
    A stealthy rustle stirs the air;
The Tigress springs, and lays him low,
    Then bears him, senseless, to her lair.

There was no sound; he gave no cry;
    The careless stars looked on serene.
The Jungle's sudden tragedy
    Remained unheard, unknown, unseen.

While on the Tower, she cried in tears,
    "Return to me, Beloved of mine,
Forgive me for my foolish fears
    Within those tender arms of thine.

"Oh, Brightest Star of all the night,
    Come back, and shed thy light on me,
And thou shalt learn, to thy delight,
    How more than kind I am to thee!"

In vain she cried, in vain she wept,
  At times in solitary woe,
Towards the inner edge she crept
  And looked, but dared not leap, below.

Before she died, three weary days
  She called in anguish on his name.
By twilight cool, or noonday blaze,
  Her luckless lover never came.

And since men rarely mount the stones
  That form the Tower's ruined stair,
It may be that her small, white bones
  Still wait in lonely silence there.

Ah, when Love comes, his wings are swift,
  His ways are full of quick surprise;
'Tis well for those who have the gift
  To seize him even as he flies!

Last Poems

The Masters

Oh, Masters, you who rule the world,
  Will you not wait with me awhile,
When swords are sheathed and sails are furled,
  And all the fields with harvest smile?
I would not waste your time for long,
  I ask you but, when you are tired,
To read how by the weak, the strong
  Are weighed and worshipped and desired.

When weary of the Mart, the Loom,
  The Withering-house, the Rifle-blocks,
The Barrack-square, the Engine-room,
  The pick-axe, ringing on the rocks,—
When tents are pitched and work is done,
  While restful twilight broods above,
By fresh-lit lamp, or dying sun,
  See in my songs how women love.

We shared your lonely watch by night,
  We knew you faithful at the helm,
Our thoughts went with you through the fight,
  That saved a soul,—or wrecked a realm.

Ah, how our hearts leapt forth to you,
  In pride and joy, when you prevailed,
And when you died, serene and true:
  —We wept in silence when you failed!

  Oh, brain, that did not gain the gold!
    Oh, arm, that could not wield the sword,
  Here is the love, that is not sold,
    Here are the hearts to hail you Lord!

You played and lost the game? What then?
  The rules are harsh and hard we know,
You, still, oh, brothers, are the men
  Whom we in secret reverence so.
Your work was waste? Maybe your share
  Lay in the hour you laughed and kissed;
Who knows but what your son shall wear
  The laurels that his father missed?

Ay, you who win, and you who lose,
  Whether you triumph,—or despair,—
When your returning footsteps choose
  The homeward track, our love is there.
For, since the world is ordered thus,
  To you the fame, the stress, the sword,
We can but wait, until to us
  You give yourselves, for our reward.

To Whaler's deck and Coral beach,
    To lonely Ranch and Frontier-Fort,
Beyond the narrow bounds of speech
    I lay the cable of my thought.
I fain would send my thanks to you,
    (Though who am I, to give you praise?)
Since what you are, and work you do,
    Are lessons for our easier ways.

    'Neath alien stars your camp-fires glow,
        I know you not,—your tents are far.
    My hope is but in song to show,
        How honoured and how dear you are.

I Shall Forget

ALTHOUGH my life, which thou hast scarred and shaken,
    Retains awhile some influence of thee,
As shells, by faithless waves long since forsaken,
    Still murmur with the music of the Sea,

I shall forget. Not thine the haunting beauty,
    Which, once beheld, for ever holds the heart,
Or, if resigned from stress of Fate or Duty,
    Takes part of life away:—the dearer part.

I gave thee love; thou gavest but Desire.
    Ah, the delusion of that summer night!
Thy soul vibrated at the rate of Fire;
    Mine, with the rhythm of the waves of Light.

It is my love for thee that I regret,
Not thee, thyself, and hence,—I shall forget!

The Lament of Yasmini, the Dancing-Girl

Ah, what hast thou done with that Lover of mine?
  The Lover who only cared for thee?
Mine for a handful of nights, and thine
  For the Nights that Are and the Days to Be,
The scent of the Champa lost its sweet—
  So sweet it was in the Times that Were!—
Since His alone, of the numerous feet
  That climb my steps, have returned not there.
    Ahi, Yasmini, return not there!

Art thou yet athrill at the touch of His hand,
  Art thou still athirst for His waving hair?
Nay, passion thou never couldst understand,
  Life's heights and depths thou wouldst never dare.
The Great Things left thee untouched, unmoved,
  The Lesser Things had thy constant care.
Ah, what hast thou done with the Lover I loved,
  Who found me wanting, and thee so fair?
    Ahi, Yasmini, He found her fair!

Nay, nay, the greatest of all was thine;
  The love of the One whom I craved for so,

But much I doubt if thou couldst divine
   The Grace and Glory of Love, or know
The worth of the One whom thine arms embraced.
   I may misjudge thee, but who can tell?
So hard it is, for the one displaced,
   To weigh the worth of a rival's spell.
      Ahi, Yasmini, thy rival's spell!

And Thou, whom I loved: have the seasons brought
   That fair content, which allured Thee so?
Is it all that Thy delicate fancy wrought?
   Yasmini wonders; she may not know.
Yet never the Stars desert the sky,
   To fade away in the desolate Dawn,
But Yasmini watches their glory die,
   And mourns for her own Bright Star withdrawn.
      Ahi, Yasmini, the lonely dawn!

Ah, never the lingering gold dies down
   In a sunset flare of resplendent light,
And never the palm-tree's feathery crown
   Uprears itself to the shadowy night,
But Yasmini thinks of those evenings past,
   When she prayed the glow of the glimmering West
To vanish quickly, that night, at last,
   Might bring Thee back to her waiting breast.
      Ahi, Yasmini, how sweet that rest!

Yet I would not say that I always weep;
   The force, that made such a desperate thing
Of my love for Thee, has not fallen asleep,
   The blood still leaps, and the senses sing,
While other passion has oft availed.
   (Other Love— Ah, my One, forgive!—)
To aid, when Churus and Opium failed;—
   I could not suffer so much and live.
      Ahi, Yasmini, who had to live!

Nay, why should I say "Forgive" to Thee?
   To whom my lovers and I are naught,
Who granted some passionate nights to me,
   Then rose and left me with never a thought!
And yet, ah, yet, for those Nights that Were,
   Thy passive limbs and thy loose loved hair,
I would pay, as I *have* paid, all these days,
   With the love that kills and the thought that slays.
      Ahi, Yasmini, thy youth it slays!

The youthful widow, with shaven hair,
   Whose senses ache for the love of a man,
The young Priest, knowing that women are fair,
   Who stems his longing as best he can,
These suffer not as I suffer for Thee;
   For the Soul desires what the senses crave,
There will never be pleasure or peace for me,

Since He who wounded, alone could save.
Ahi, Yasmini, He will not save!

The torchlight flares, and the lovers lean
　　Towards Yasmini, with yearning eyes,
Who dances, wondering what they mean,
　　And gives cold kisses, and scant replies.
They talk of Love, she withholds the name,—
　　(Love came to her as a Flame of Fire!)
From things that are only a weary shame;
　　Trivial Vanity;—light Desire.
　　　　Ahi, Yasmini, the light Desire!

Yasmini bends to the praise of men,
　　And looks in the mirror, upon her hand,[1]
To curse the beauty that failed her then—
　　Ah, none of her lovers can understand!
How her whole life hung on that beauty's power,
　　The spell that waned at the final test,
The charm that paled in the vital hour,—
　　Which won so many,—yet lost the best!
　　　　Ahi, Yasmini, who lost the best!

She leaves the dancing to reach the roof,
　　With the lover who claims the passing hour,
Her lips are his, but her eyes aloof
　　While the starlight falls in a silver shower.

[1] Indian women wear a small mirror in a ring on their thumbs.

Let him take what pleasure, what love, he **may**,
　He, too, will suffer ere life be spent,—
But Yasmini's soul has wandered away
　To join the Lover, who came,—and went!
　　Ahi, Yasmini, He came,—and went!

Among the Rice Fields

She was fair as a Passion-flower,
    (But little of love he knew.)
Her lucent eyes were like amber wine,
    And her eyelids stained with blue.

He called them the Gates of Fair Desire,
    And the Lakes where Beauty lay,
But I looked into them once, and saw
    The eyes of Beasts of Prey.

He praised her teeth, that were small and white
    As lilies upon his lawn,
While I remembered a tiger's fangs
    That met in a speckled fawn.

She had her way; a lover the more,
    And I had a friend the less.
For long there was nothing to do but wait
    And suffer his happiness.

But now I shall choose the sharpest Kriss
    And nestle it in her breast,
For dead, he is drifting down to sea,
    And his own hand wrought his rest.

The Bride

Beat on the Tom-toms, and scatter the flowers,
    Jasmine, Hibiscus, vermilion and white,
This is the day, and the Hour of Hours,
    Bring forth the Bride for her Lover's delight.
Maidens no more, as a maiden shall claim her,
    Near, in his Mystery, draweth Desire.
Who, if she waver a moment, shall blame her?
    She is a flower, and love is a fire.
            Choti Tinchaurya syani hogayi! [1]

Give her the anklets, the rings and the necklace,
    Darken her eyelids with delicate Art,
Heighten the beauty, so youthful and fleckless,
    By the Gods favoured, oh, Bridegroom thou art!
Twine in thy fingers her fingers so slender,
    Circle together the Mystical Fire,
Bridegroom,—a whisper—be gentle and tender,
    Choti Tinchaurya knows not desire.
            Abhi Tinchaurya syani hogayi!

[1] *Anglice:* Little Tinchaurya has grown up.

Bring forth the silks and the veil that shall cover
    Beauty, till yesterday, careless and wild,
Red are her lips for the kiss of a lover,
    Ripe are her breasts for the lips of a child.
Centre and Shrine of Mysterious Power,
    Chalice of Pleasure and Rose of Delight,
Shyly aware of the swift-coming hour,
    Waiting the shade and the silence of night,
            Choti Tinchaurya syani hogayi!

Still must the Bridegroom his longing dissemble,
    Longing to loosen the silk-woven cord,
Ah, how his fingers will flutter and tremble,
    Fingers well skilled with the bridle and sword.
Thine is his valour, oh, Bride, and his beauty,
    Thine to possess and re-issue again,
Such is thy tender and passionate duty,
    Licit thy pleasure and honoured thy pain.
            Choti Tinchaurya syani hogayi!

Choti Tinchaurya, lovely and tender,
    Still all unbroken to sorrow and strife.
Come to the Bridegroom who, silk-clad and slender,
    Brings thee the Honour and Burden of Life.
Bidding farewell to thy light-hearted playtime,
    Worship thy Lover with fear and delight,
Art thou not ever, though slave of his daytime,
    Choti Tinchaurya, queen of his night?
            Choti Tinchaurya syani hogayi!

Unanswered

Something compels me, somewhere. Yet I see
No clear command in Life's long mystery.

Oft have I flung myself beside my horse,
    To drink the water from the roadside mire,
And felt the liquid through my being course,
    Stilling the anguish of my thirst's desire.

A simple want; so easily allayed;
After the burning march; water and shade.

Also I lay against the loved one's heart
    Finding fulfilment in that resting-place,
Feeling my longing, quenched, was but a part
    Of nature's ceaseless striving for the race.

But now, I know not what they would with me;
Matter or Force or God, if Gods there be.

I wait; I question; Nature heeds me not.
    She does but urge in answer to my prayer,
"Arise and do!" Alas, she adds not what;
    "Arise and go!" Alas, she says not where!

The Net of Memory

I cast the Net of Memory,
Man's torment and delight,
Over the level Sands of Youth
That lay serenely bright,
Their tranquil gold at times submerged
In the Spring Tides of Love's Delight.

The Net brought up, in silver gleams,
Forgotten truth and fancies fair:
Like opal shells, small happy facts
Within the Net entangled were
With the red coral of his lips,
The waving seaweed of his hair.

We were so young; he was so fair.

The Cactus Thicket

"THE Atlas summits were veiled in purple gloom,
   But a golden moon above rose clear and free.
The cactus thicket was ruddy with scarlet bloom
   Where, through the silent shadow, he came to me."

"All my sixteen summers were but for this,
   That He should pass, and, pausing, find me fair.
You Stars! bear golden witness! My lips were his;
   I would not live till others have fastened there."

"Oh, take me, Death, ere ever the charm shall fade,
   Ah, close these eyes, ere ever the dream grow dim.
I welcome thee with rapture, and unafraid,
   Even as yesternight I welcomed Him."

    *   *   *   *   *   *

"Not now, Impatient one; it well may be
   That ten moons hence I shall return for thee."

Song of the Peri

BEAUTY, the Gift of Gifts, I give to thee.
   Pleasure and love shall spring around thy feet
As through the lake the lotuses arise
   Pinkly transparent and divinely sweet.

I give thee eyes aglow like morning stars,
   Delicate brows, a mist of sable tresses,
That all the journey of thy life may be
   Lit up by love and softened by caresses.

For those who once were proud and softly bred
   Shall, kneeling, wait thee as thou passest by,
They who were pure shall stretch forth eager hands
   Crying, "Thy pity, Lord, before we die!"

And one shall murmur, "If the sun at dawn
   Shall open and caress a happy flower,
What blame to him, although the blossom fade
   In the full splendour of his noontide power?"

And one, "If aloes close together grow
   It well may chance a plant shall wounded be,

Pierced by the thorntips of another's leaves,
    Thus am I hurt unconsciously by thee."

For some shall die and many more shall sin,
    Suffering for thy sake till seven times seven,
Because of those most perfect lips of thine
    Which held the power to make or mar their heaven.

And though thou givest back but cruelty,
    Their love, persistent, shall not heed nor care,
All those whose ears are fed with blame of thee
    Shall say, "It may be so, but he was fair."

Ay, those who lost the whole of youth for thee,
    Made early and for ever, shamed and sad,
Shall sigh, re-living some sweet memory,
    "Ah, once it was his will to make me glad."

Thy nights shall be as bright as summer days,
    The sequence of thy sins shall seem as duty,
Since I have given thee, oh, Gift of Gifts!—
    The pale perfection of unrivalled beauty.

Though in My Firmament Thou Wilt Not Shine

Talk not, my Lord, of unrequited love,
   Since love requites itself most royally.
Do we not live but by the sun above,
   And takes he any heed of thee or me?

Though in my firmament thou wilt not shine,
   Thy glory, as a Star, is none the less.
Oh, Rose, though all unplucked by hand of mine,
   Still am I debtor to thy loveliness.

The Convert

The sun was hot on the tamarind trees,
   Their shadows shrivelled and shrank.
No coolness came on the off-shore breeze
   That rattled the scrub on the bank.
She stretched her appealing arms to me,
Uplifting the Flagon of Love to me,
Till—great indeed was my unslaked thirst—
   I paused, I stooped, and I drank!

I went with my foe to the edge of the crater,—
   But one to return, we knew,—
The lava's heat had never been greater
   Than the ire between us two.
He flung back his head and he mocked at me,
He spat unspeakable words at me,
Our eyes met, and our knives met,
   I saw red, and I slew!

Such were my deeds when my youth was hot,
   And force was new to my hand,
With many more that I tell thee not,
   Well known in my native land.

These show thy Christ when thou prayest to Him,
He too was a man thou sayest of Him,
Therefore He, when I reach His feet,
   Will remember, and understand.

Ashore

Out I came from the dancing-place:
The night-wind met me face to face—

A wind off the harbour, cold and keen,
"I know," it whistled, "where thou hast been."

A faint voice fell from the stars above—
"Thou? whom we lighted to shrines of Love!"

I found when I reached my lonely room
A faint sweet scent in the unlit gloom.

And this was the worst of all to bear,
For someone had left white lilac there.

The flower you loved, in times that were.

Yasin Khan

Ay, thou hast found thy kingdom, Yasin Khan,
   Thy fathers' pomp and power are thine, at last.
No more the rugged roads of Khorasan,
   The scanty food and tentage of the past!

Wouldst thou make war? thy followers know no fear,
   Where shouldst thou lead them but to victory?
Wouldst thou have love? thy soft-eyed slaves draw near,
   Eager to drain thy strength away from thee.

My thoughts drag backwards to forgotten days,
   To scenes etched deeply on my heart by pain;
The thirsty marches, ambuscades, and frays,
   The hostile hills, the burnt and barren plain.

Hast thou forgotten how one night was spent,
   Crouched in a camel's carcase by the road,
Along which Akbar's soldiers, scouting, went,
   And he himself, all unsuspecting, rode.

Did we not waken one despairing dawn,
   Attacked in front, cut off in rear, by snow.

Till, like a tiger leaping on a fawn,
  Half of the hill crashed down upon the foe?

Once, as thou mournd'st thy lifeless brother's fate,
  The red tears falling from thy shattered wrist,
A spent Waziri, forceful still, in hate,
  Covered thy heart, ten paces off,—and missed!

Ahi, men thrust a worn and dinted sword
  Into a velvet-scabbarded repose;
The gilded pageants that salute thee Lord
  Cover *one* sorrow-rusted heart, God knows.

Ah, to exchange this wealth of idle days
  For one cold reckless night of Khorasan!
To crouch once more before the camp-fire blaze
  That lit the lonely eyes of Yasin Khan.

To watch the starlight glitter on the snows,
  The plain stretched round us like a waveless sea,
Waiting until thy weary lids should close
  To slip my furs and spread them over thee.

How the wind howled about the lonely pass,
  While the faint snowshine of that plateau'd space
Lit, where it lay upon the frozen grass,
  The mournful, tragic beauty of thy face.

Thou hast enough caressed the scented hair
  Of these soft-breasted girls who waste thee so;
Hast thou not sons for every adult year?
  Let us arise, O Yasin Khan, and go!

Let us escape from out these prison bars
  To gain the freedom of an open sky,
Thy soul and mine, alone beneath the stars,
  Intriguing danger, as in days gone by.

Nay; there is no returning, Yasin Khan.
  The white peaks ward the passes, as of yore,
The wind sweeps o'er the wastes of Khorasan;—
  But thou and I go thitherward no more.

Close, ah, too close, the bitter knowledge clings,
  We may not follow where my fancies yearn.
The years go hence, and wild and lovely things,
  Their own, go with them, never to return.

Khristna and His Flute
(Translation by Moolchand)

Be still, my heart, and listen,
   For sweet and yet acute
I hear the wistful music
   Of Khristna and his flute.
Across the cool, blue evenings,
   Throughout the burning days,
Persuasive and beguiling,
   He plays and plays and plays.

Ah, none may hear such music
   Resistant to its charms,
The household work grows weary,
   And cold the husband's arms.
I must arise and follow,
   To seek, in vain pursuit,
The blueness and the distance,
   The sweetness of that flute!

In linked and liquid sequence,
   The plaintive notes dissolve

Divinely tender secrets
  That none but he can solve.
Oh, Khristna, I am coming,
  I can no more delay.
"My heart has flown to join thee,"
  How shall my footsteps stay?

Beloved, such thoughts have peril;
  The wish is in my mind
That I had fired the jungle,
  And left no leaf behind,—
Burnt all bamboos to ashes,
  And made their music mute,—
To save thee from the magic
  Of Khristna and his flute.

Song of Jasoda

Had I been young I could have claimed to fold thee
    For many days against my eager breast;
But, as things are, how can I hope to hold thee
    Once thou hast wakened from this fleeting rest?

Clear shone the moonlight, so that thou couldst find me,
    Yet not so clear that thou couldst see my face,
Where in the shadow of the palms behind me
    I waited for thy steps, for thy embrace.

What reck I now my morning life was lonely?
    For widowed feet the ways are always rough.
Though thou hast come to me at sunset only,
    Still thou hast come, my Lord, it is enough.

Ah, mine no more the glow of dawning beauty,
    The fragrance and the dainty gloss of youth,
Worn by long years of solitude and duty,
    I have no bloom to offer thee in truth.

Yet, since these eyes of mine have never wandered,
    Still may they gleam with long forgotten light.

Since in no wanton way my youth was squandered,
  Some sense of youth still clings to me to-night.

Thy lips are fresh as dew on budding roses,
  The gold of dawn still lingers in thy hair,
While the abandonment of sleep discloses
  How every attitude of youth is fair.

Thou art so pale, I hardly dare caress thee,
  Too brown my fingers show against the white.
Ahi, the glory, that I should possess thee,
  Ahi, the grief, but for a single night!

The tulip tree has pallid golden flowers
  That grow more rosy as their petals fade;
Such is the splendour of my evening hours
  Whose time of youth was wasted in the shade.

I shall not wait to see to-morrow's morning,
  Too bright the golden dawn for me,—too bright,—
How could I bear thine eyes' unconscious scorning
  Of what so pleased thee in the dimmer light?

It may be wine had brought some brief illusion,
  Filling thy brain with rainbow fantasy,
Or youth, with moonlight, making sweet collusion,
  Threw an alluring glamour over me.

Therefore I leave thee softly, to awaken
  When the first sun rays warm thy blue-veined breast,
Smiling and all unknowing I have taken
  The poppied drink that brings me endless rest.

Thus would I have thee rise; thy fancy laden
  With the vague sweetness of the bygone night,
Thinking of me as some consenting maiden,
  Whose beauty blossomed first for thy delight.

While I, if any kindly visions hover
  Around the silence of my last repose,
Shall dream of thee, my pale and radiant lover,
  Who made my life so lovely at its close!

Song of Ramesram Temple Girl

Now is the season of my youth,
   Not thus shall I always be,
Listen, dear Lord, thou too art young,
   Take thy pleasure with me.
My hair is straight as the falling rain,
   And fine as the morning mist,
I am a rose awaiting thee
   That none have touched or kissed.

        Do as thou wilt with mine and me,
          Beloved, I only pray,
        Follow the promptings of thy youth.
        Let there be no delay!

A leaf that flutters upon the bough,
   A moment, and it is gone,—
A bubble amid the fountain spray,—
   Ah, pause, and think thereon;
For such is youth and its passing **bloom**
   That wait for thee this hour,
If aught in thy heart incline to me
   Ah, stoop and pluck thy flower!

Come, my Lord, to the temple shade,
  Where cooling fountains play,
If aught in thy heart incline to love
  Let there be no delay!

Many shall faint with love of me
  And I shall slake their thirst,
But Fate has brought thee hither to-day
  That thou shouldst be the first.
Old, so old are the temple-walls,
  Love is older than they;
But I am the short-lived temple rose,
  Blooming for thee to-day.

Thine am I, Prince, and only thine,
  What is there more to say?
If aught in thy heart incline to love
  Let there be no delay!

The Rao of Ilore

I was sold to the Rao of Ilore,
  Slender and tall was he.
When his litter carried him down the street
  I peeped through the thatch to see.
        Ah, the eyes of the Rao of Ilore,
          My lover that was to be!

The hair that lay on his youthful brow
  Was curled like an ocean wave;
His eyes were lit with a tender smile,
  But his lips were soft and grave.
For sake of these things I was still with joy
  When the silver coins were paid,
And they took me up to the Palace gates,
  Delighted and unafraid.
        Ah, the eyes of the Rao of Ilore,
          May never their brilliance fade!

So near was I to the crown of life!
  Ten thousand times, alas!
The Diwan leant from the latticed hall,
  Looked down and saw me pass.

He begged for me from the Rao of Ilore,
   Who answered, "She is thine,
Thou wert ever more than a father to me,
   And thy desires are mine."
          Ah, the eyes of the Rao of Ilore
          That never had looked in mine!

My years were spent in the Diwan's Courts,
   My youth died down that day.
For sake of thine own content of mind
   My lost beloved, I pray
That never my Lord a love may know
   Like that he threw away.
          Ah, the eyes of the Rao of Ilore,
          Who threw my life away!

To M. C. N.

Thou hast no wealth, nor any pride of power,
    Thy life is offered on affection's altar.
Small sacrifices claim thee, hour by hour,
    Yet on the tedious path thou dost not falter.

To the unknowing, well thy days might seem
    Circled by solitude and tireless duty,
Yet is thy soul made radiant by a dream
    Of delicate and rainbow-coloured beauty.

Never a flower trembles in the wind,
    Never a sunset lingers on the sea,
But something of its fragrance joins thy mind,
    Some sparkle of its light remains with thee.

Thus when thy spirit enters on its rest,
Thy lips shall say, "I too have known the best!"

Disappointment

Oh, come, Beloved, before my beauty fades,
    Pity the sorrow of my loneliness.
I am a Rosebush that the Cypress shades,
    No sunbeams find or lighten my distress.

Daily I watch the waning of my bloom.
    Ah, piteous fading of a thing so fair!
While Fate, remorseless, weaving at her loom,
    Twines furtive silver in my twisted hair.

This noon I watched a tremulous fading rose
    Rise on the wind to court a butterfly.
"One speck of pollen, ere my petals close,
    Bring me one touch of love before I die!"

But the gay butterfly, who had the power
    To grant, refused, flew far across the dell,
And, as he fertilised a younger flower,
    The petals of the rose, defrauded, fell.

Such was my fate, thou hast not come to me,
    Thine eyes are absent, and thy voice is mute,

Though I am slim, as this Papaya tree,
   With breasts out-pointing, even as its fruit.

Beauty was mine, it brought me no caress,
   My lips were red, yet there were none to taste,
I saw my youth consume in loneliness,
   And all the fervour of my heart run waste.

While I still hoped that Thou wouldst come to me,
   I and the garden waited for their Lord.
Here He will rest, beneath this Champa tree;
   Hence, all ye spike-set grasses from the sward!

In this cool rillet I shall bathe His feet,
   Come, rounded pebbles from a smoother shore.
This is the honey that His lips will eat,
   Hasten, O bees, enhance the amber store!

Ripen, ye Custard Apples, round and fair,
   Practice your songs, O Bulbuls, on the bough,
Surely some sweeter sweetness haunts the air;
   Maybe His feet draw near us, even now!

Disperse, ye fireflies, clustered on the palm,
   Love heeds no lamp, he welcomes moonless skies:
Soon shall ye find, O stars, serene and calm,
   Your sparkling rivals in my lover's eyes!

Closely I wove my leafy Jasmine bowers,
   Hoping to hide my pleasure and my shame,

Where the Lantana's indecisive flowers
   Vary from palest rose to orange flame.

Ay, there were lovely hours, 'neath fern and palm,
   Almost my aching longing I forgot.
White nights of silence, noons of golden calm,
   All past, all wasted, since Thou camest not!

Night after night the Champa trees distilled
   Their cruel sweetness on the careless air.
Noon after noon I watched the Bulbuls build,
   And saw with hungry eyes the Sun-birds pair.

None came, and none will come; no use to wait,—
   Youth's fragrance dies, its tender light dies down.
I will arise, before it grows too late,
   And seek the noisy brilliance of the town.

These many waiting years I longed for gold,
   Now must I needs console me with alloy.
Before this beauty fades, this pulse grows cold,
   I may not love, I will at least enjoy!

Farewell, my Solitude of scented flowers,
   Across whose glades the emerald parrots gleam,
Haunt of false hope, and home of wasted hours,
   I am awake, at last,—Guard thou the dream!

On Pilgrimage

Oh, youthful bearer of my palanquin,
  Thy glossy hair lies loosened on thy neck,
The "tears of labour" gem thy velvet skin,
  Whose even texture knows no other fleck.

Thy slender shoulder strains beneath my weight;
  Too fair thou art for work, sweet slave of mine.
Would that this idle breast, reversing fate,
  A willing serf to love, supported thine!

I smell the savage scent of sun-warmed fur
  Close in the Jungle, musky, hot and sweet.—
The air comes from thy shoulder, even as myrrh,
  Would we were as the panthers, free to meet.

The Temple road is steep; I grieve to see
  Thy slender ankles bruised among the clods.
Oh, my Beloved, if I might worship thee!
  Beauty is greater far than all the Gods.

The Rice-Boat

I slept upon the Rice-boat
    That, reef protected, lay
At anchor, where the palm-trees
    Infringe upon the bay.
The windless air was heavy
    With cinnamon and rose,
The midnight calm seemed waiting,
    Too fateful for repose.

One joined me on the Rice-boat
    With wild and waving hair,
Whose vivid words and laughter
    Awoke the silent air.
Oh, beauty, bare and shining,
    Fresh washen in the bay,
One well may love by moonlight
    What one would not love by day!

Above among the cordage
    The night wind hardly stirred,
The lapping of the ripples
    Was all the sound we heard.

Love reigned upon the Rice-boat,
    And Peace controlled the sea,
The spirit's consolation,
    The senses' ecstasy.

Though many things and mighty
    Are furthered in the West,
The ancient Peace has vanished
    Before To-day's unrest.
For how among their striving,
    Their gold, their lust, their drink,
Shall men find time for dreaming
    Or any space to think?

Think not I scorn the Science
    That lightens human pain;
Though man's reliance often
    Is placed on it in vain.
Maybe the long endeavour,
    The patience and the strife,
May some day solve the riddle,
    The Mystery of Life.

Perchance I do not value
    Things Western as I ought,
The trains,—that take us, whither?
    The ships,—that reach, what port?
To me it seems but chaos
    Of greed and haste and rage,

The endless, aimless, motion
    Of squirrels in a cage.

Here, where some ruined temple
    In solitude decays,
With carven walls still hallowed
    With prayers of bygone days,
Here, where the coral outcrops
    Make "flowers of the sea,"
The olden Peace yet lingers,
    In hushed serenity.

Ah, silent, silver moonlight,
    Whose charm impartial falls
On tanks of sacred water
    And squalid city walls,
Whose mystic whiteness hallows
    The lowest and the least,
To thee men owe the glamour
    That draws them to the East.

And as this azure water,
    Unflecked by wave or foam,
Conceals in its tranquillity
    The dreaded white shark's home,
So if love be illusion
    I ask the dream to stay,
Content to love by moonlight
    What I might not love by day.

Lallji, My Desire

"This is no time for saying 'no'"
  Were thy last words to me,
And yet my lips refused the kiss
  They might have given thee.
            How could I know
            That thou wouldst go
            To sleep so far from me?

They took thee to the Burning-Ghat,
  Oh, Lallji, my desire.
And now a faint and lonely flame
  Uprises from the pyre.
The thin grey smoke in spirals drifts
  Across the opal sky.
Would that I were a wife of thine,
  And thus with thee could die!
            How could I know
            That thou wouldst go,
            Oh, Lallji, my desire?
            The lips I missed
            The flames have kissed
            Upon the Sandal pyre.

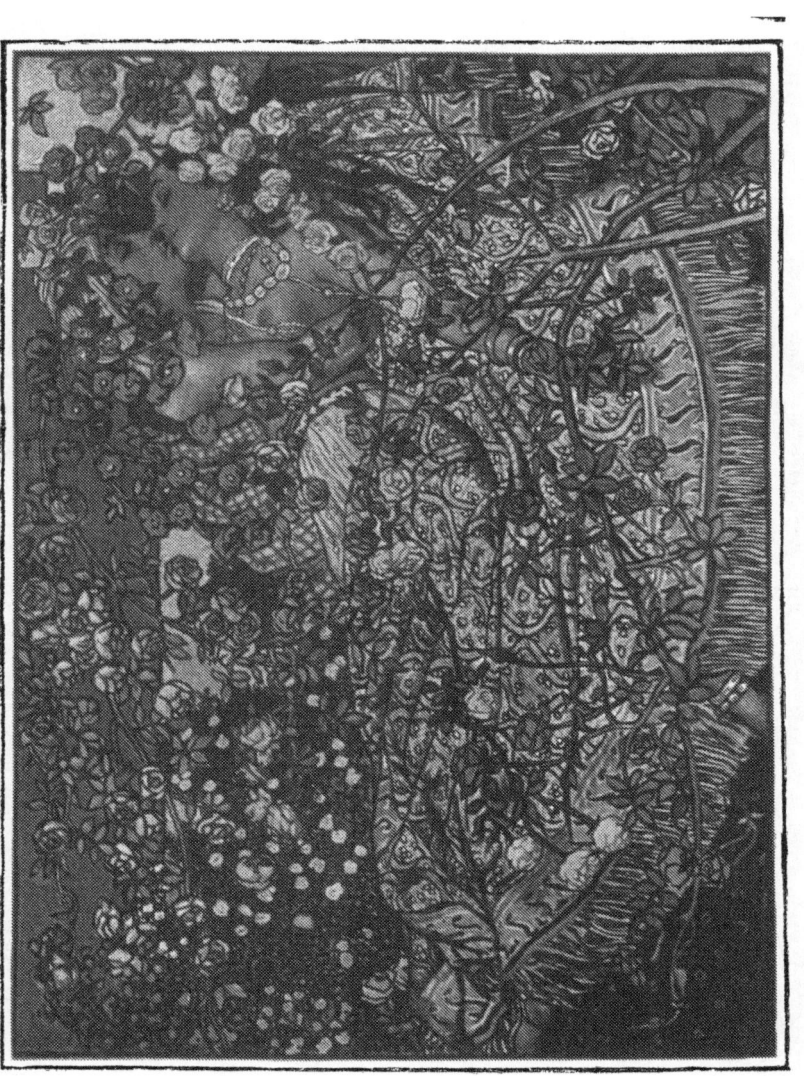

Lallji, My Desire

If one should meet me with a knife
    And cut my heart in twain,
Then would he see the smoke arise
    From every severed vein.
Such is the burning, inward fire,
    The anguish of my pain,
For my Beloved, whose dying lips
    Implored a kiss—in vain!
        How could I know
        That thou wouldst go,
        Oh, Lallji, my desire?
        Too young thou art
        To lay thy heart
        Upon the Sandal pyre.

Thy wife awaits her coming child;
    What were a child to me,
If I might take thee in these arms
    And face the flames with thee?
The priests are chanting round the pyre,
    At dusk they will depart
And leave to thee thy lonely rest,
    To me my lonelier heart.
        How could I know
        Thou lovedst me so?
        Upon the Sandal pyre
        He lies forsaken.
        The flames have taken
        My Lallji, my desire!

Rutland Gate

His back is bent and his lips are blue,
    Shivering out in the wet:
"Here's a florin, my man, for you,
    Go and get drunk and forget!"

Right in the midst of a Christian land,
    Rotted with wealth and ease,
Broken and dragged they let him stand
    Till his feet on the pavement freeze.

God leaves His poor in His vicars' care,
    For He hears the church-bells ring,
His ears are buzzing with constant prayer
    And the hymns His people sing.

Can His pity picture the anguish here,
    Can He see, through a London fog,
The man who has worked "nigh seventy year"
    To die the death of a dog?

No one heeds him, the crowds pass on.
    Why does he want to live?
"Take this florin, and get you gone,
    Go and get drunk,—and forgive!"

Atavism

Deep in the jungle vast and dim,
    That knew not a white man's feet,
I smelt the odour of sun-warmed fur,
    Musky, savage and sweet.

Far it was from the huts of men
    And the grass where Sambur feed;
I threw a stone at a Kadapu tree
    That bled as a man might bleed.

Scent of fur and colour of blood:—
    And the long dead instincts rose,
I followed the lure of my season's mate,—
    And flew, bare-fanged, at my foes.

      *   *   *

Pale days: and a league of laws
    Made by the whims of men.
Would I were back with my furry cubs
    In the dusk of a jungle den.

Middle-Age

The sins of Youth are hardly sins,
  So frank they are and free.
'T is but when Middle-age begins
  We need morality.

Ah, pause and weigh this bitter truth:
  That Middle-age, grown cold,
No comprehension has of Youth,
  No pity for the Old.

Youth, with his half-divine mistakes,
  She never can forgive,
So much she hates his charm which makes
  Worth while the life we live.

She scorns Old Age, whose tolerance
  And calm, well-balanced mind
(Knowing how crime is born of chance)
  Can pardon all mankind.

Yet she, alas! has all the power
  Of strength and place and gold,

Man's every act, through every hour,
    Is by her laws controlled.

All things she grasps with sordid hands
    And weighs in tarnished scales.
She neither feels, nor understands,
    And yet her will prevails!

Cold-blooded vice and careful sin,
    Gold-lust, blind selfishness,—
The shortest, cheapest way to win
    Some, worse than cheap, success.

Such are her attributes and aims,
    Yet meekly we obey,
While she to guide and order claims
    All issues of the day.

You seek for honour, friendship, truth?
    Let Middle-age be banned!
Go, for warm-hearted acts, to Youth;
    To Age,—to understand!

The Jungle Flower

Ah, the cool silence of the shaded hours,
The scent and colour of the jungle flowers!

Thou are one of the jungle flowers, strange and fierce and fair,
  Palest amber, perfect lines, and scented with champa flower.
Lie back and frame thy face in the gloom of thy loosened hair;
  Sweet thou art and loved—ay, loved—for an hour.

But thought flies far, ah, far, to another breast,
  Whose whiteness breaks to the rose of a twin pink flower,
Where wind the azure veins that my lips caressed
  When Fate was gentle to me for a too-brief hour.

There is my spirit's home and my soul's abode,
The rest are only inns on the traveller's road.

From Behind the Lattice

I SEE your red-golden hair and know
   How white the hidden skin must be,
Though sun-kissed face and fingers show
The fervour of the noon-day glow,
   The keenness of the sea.

My longing fancies ebb and flow,
   Still circling constant unto this;
My great desire (ah, whisper low)
To plant on thy forbidden snow
   The rosebud of a kiss.

The scarlet flower would spread and grow,
   Your whiteness change and flush,
(Be still, my reckless heart, beat slow,
'T is but a dream that stirs thee so!)
   To one transparent blush.

Wings

Was it worth while to forego our wings
    To gain these dextrous hands?
Truly they fashion us wonderful things
    As the fancy of man demands.

But—to fly! to sail through the lucid air
    From crest to violet crest
Of these great grey mountains, quartz-veined and bare,
    Where the white clouds gather and rest.

Even to flutter from flower to flower,—
    To skim the tops of the trees,—
In the roseate light of a sun-setting hour
    To drift on a sea-going breeze.

Ay, the hands have marvellous skill
    To create us curious things,—
Baubles, playthings, weapons to kill,—
    But—I would we had chosen wings!

Song of the Parao (Camping-Ground)

Heart, my heart, thou hast found thy home!
    From gloom and sorrow thou hast come forth,
Thou who wast foolish, and sought to roam
    'Neath the cruel stars of the frozen North.

Thou hast returned to thy dear delights;
    The golden glow of the quivering days,
The silver silence of tropical nights,
    No more to wander in alien ways.

        Here, each star is a well-loved friend;
        To me and my heart at the journey's end.

These are my people, and this my land,
    I hear the pulse of her secret soul.
This is the life that I understand,
    Savage and simple and sane and whole.

        Washed in the light of a clear fierce sun,—
        Heart, my heart, the journey is done.

See! the painted piece of the skies,
Where the rose-hued opal of sunset lies.

Hear the passionate Koel calling
From coral trees, where the dusk is falling.
See my people, slight limbed and tall.
The maiden's bosom they scorn to cover:
The breasts that shall call and enthral her lover,
Things of beauty, are free to all.

Free to the eyes, that think no shame
That a girl should bloom like a forest flower.
Who hold that Love is a sacred flame,—
Outward beauty a God-like dower.

Who further regard it as no disgrace
If loveliness lessen to serve the race,
Nor point the finger of jesting scorn
At her who carries the child unborn.

Ah, my heart, but we wandered far
From the light of the slanting fourfold Star!

Oh, palm-leaf thatch, where the melon thrives
Beneath the shade of the tamarind tree,
Thou coverest tranquil, graceful lives,
That want so little, that knew no haste,
Nor the bitter goad of a too-full hour;
Whose soft-eyed women are lithe and tall,
And wear no garment below the knee,
Nor veil or raiment above the waist,

But the beautiful hair, that dowers them all,
    And falls to the ground in a scented shower.

The youths return from their swift-flowing bath,
    With the swinging grace that their height allows,
Lightly climbing the river-side path,
    Their soft hair knotted above their brows.
Elephants wade the darkening river,
    Their bells, which tinkle in minor thirds,
Faintly sweet, like passionate birds
    Whose warbling wakens a sense of pain,—
Thrill through the nerves and make them quiver,—
    Heart, my heart, art thou happy again?

Here is beauty to feast thine eyes.
    Here is the land of thy long desire.
See how the delicate spirals rise
    Azure and faint from the wood-fed fire.

Where the cartmen wearily share their food,
    Ere they, by their bullocks, lie down to rest,
Heart of mine, dost thou find it good,
    This wide red road by the winds caressed?

         This lone Parao, where the fireflies light?
         These tom-toms, fretting the peace of night?

Heart, thou hast wandered and suffered much,
    Death has robbed thee, and Life betrayed,

But there is ever a solace for such
  In that they are not lightly afraid.

The strength that found them the fire to love
  Finds them also the force to forget.
Thy joy in thy dreaming lives to prove
  Thou art not mortally wounded yet.

Here, 'neath the arch of the vast, clear sky,
  Where range upon range the remote grey hills
Far in the distance recede and die,
  There is no space for thy trivial ills.

On the low horizon towards the sea,
  Faint yet vivid, the lightnings play,
The lucid air is kind as a kiss,
  The falling twilight is cool and grey.
    What has sorrow to do with thee?
    Love was cruel? Thou now art free.
    Life unkind? It has given thee this!

The Tom-Toms

Dost thou hear the tom-toms throbbing,
Like a lonely lover sobbing
For the beauty that is robbing him of all his life's delight?
Plaintive sounds, restrained, enthralling,
Seeking through the twilight falling
Something lost beyond recalling, in the darkness of the night.

Oh, my little, loved Firoza,
Come and nestle to me closer,
Where the golden-balled Mimosa makes a canopy above,
For the day, so hot and burning,
Dies away, and night, returning,
Sets thy lover's spirit yearning for thy beauty and thy love.

Soon will come the rosy warning
Of the bright relentless morning,
When, thy soft caresses scorning, I shall leave thee in the shade.
All the day my work must chain me,
And its weary bonds restrain me,
For I may not re-attain thee till the light begins to fade.

But at length the long day endeth,
As the cool of night descendeth
His last strength thy lover spendeth in returning to thy breast,
Where beneath the Babul nightly,
While the planets shimmer whitely,
And the fire-flies glimmer brightly, thou shalt give him love and rest.

Far away, across the distance,
The quick-throbbing drums' persistence
Shall resound, with soft insistence, in the pauses of delight,
Through the sequence of the hours,
While the starlight and the flowers
Consecrate this love of ours, in the Temple of the Night.

Written in Cananore

I

WHO was it held that Love was soothing or sweet?
Mine is a painful fire, at its whitest heat.

Who said that Beauty was ever a gentle joy?
Thine is a sword that flashes but to destroy.

Though mine eyes rose up from thy Beauty's banquet, calm and refreshed,
My lips, that were granted naught, can find no rest.

My soul was linked with thine, through speech and silent hours,
As the sound of two soft flutes combined, or the scent of sister flowers.

But the body, that wretched slave of the Sultan, Mind,
Who follows his master ever, but far behind,

Nothing was granted him, and every rebellious cell
Rises up with angry protest, "It is not well!
Night is falling; thou hast departed; I am alone;

And the Last Sweetness of Love thou hast not given—I have not known!"

II

Somewhere, oh, My Beloved One, the house is standing,
Waiting for thee and me; for our first caresses.
It may be a river-boat, or a wave-washed landing,
The shade of a tree in the jungle's dim recesses,
    Some far-off mountain tent, ill-pitched and lonely,
    Or the naked vault of the purple heavens only.

But the Place is waiting there; till the Hour shall show it,
And our footsteps, following Fate, find it and know it.

Where we shall worship the greatest of all the Gods in his pomp and power,—
I sometimes think that I shall not care to survive that hour!

Feroke

The rice-birds fly so white, so silver white,
    The velvet rice-flats lie so emerald green,
My heart inhales, with sorrowful delight,
    The sweet and poignant sadness of the scene.

The swollen tawny river seeks the sea,
    Its hungry waters, never satisfied,
Beflecked with fallen log and torn-up tree,
    Engulf the fisher-huts on either side.

The current brought a stranger yesterday,
    And laid him on the sand beneath a palm,
His worn young face was partly torn away,
    His eyes, that saw the world no more, were calm.

We could not close his eyelids, stiff with blood,—
    But, oh, my brother, I had changed with thee!
For I am still tormented in the flood,
    Whilst thou hast done thy work, and reached the sea.

My Desire

FATE has given me many a gift
   To which men most aspire,
Lovely, precious and costly things,
   But not my heart's desire.

Many a man has a secret dream
   Of where his soul would be.
Mine is a low verandah'd house
   In a tope beside the sea.

Over the roof tall palms should wave,
   Swaying from side to side,
Every night we should fall asleep
   To the rhythm of the tide.

The dawn should be gay with song of birds,
   And the stir of fluttering wings.
Surely the joy of life is hid
   In simple and tender things!

At eve the waves would shimmer with gold
   In the rosy sunset rays,

Emerald velvet flats of rice
    Would rest the landward gaze.

A boat must rock at the laterite steps
    In a reef-protected pool,
For we should sail through the starlit night
    When the winds were calm and cool.

I am so tired of all this world,
    Its folly and fret and care.
Find me a little scented home
    Amongst thy loosened hair.

Give me a soft and secret place
    Against thine amber breast,
Where, hidden away from all mankind,
    My soul may come to rest.

Many a man has a secret dream
    Of where his life might be;
Mine is a lovely, lonely place
    With sunshine and the sea.

Sher Afzul

This was the tale Sher Afzul told to me,
   While the spent camels bubbled on their knees,
And ruddy camp-fires twinkled through the gloom
   Sweet with the fragrance from the Sinjib trees.

I had a friend who lay, condemned to death
   In gaol for murder, wholly innocent,
Yet caught in webs of luckless circumstance;—
   Thou know'st how lies, of good and ill intent,

Cluster like flies around a justice-court,
   Wheel within wheel, revolving screw on screw;—
But from his prison he escaped and fled,
   Keeping his liberty a night or two

Among the lonely hills, where, shackled still,
   He braved a village, seeking for a file
To loose his irons; alas! he lost his life
   Through the base sweetness of a woman's smile.

Lovely she was, and young, who gave the youth
   Kind words, and promised succor and repose,

Till on the quilt of false security
    He found exhausted sleep; but, ere he rose,

Entered the guards, brought by her messenger.
    Thus was he captured, slain, and on her breast
Soon shone the guerdon of her treachery,
    The price of blood; in gold made manifest.

I might have killed her? Brave men have died thus.
    Revenge demanded keener punishment.
So I walked softly on those lilac hills,
    Touching my *rhibab* lightly as I went.

I found her fair: 'twas no unpleasant task
    In the young spring-time when the fruit-trees flower,
To pass her door, and pause, and pass again,
    Shading mine eyes against her beauty's power.

Warmly I wooed her, while the almond trees
    Broke into fragile clouds of rosy snow.
Her dawning passion feared her lord's return,
    Ever she pleaded softly, "Let us go."

But I spoke tenderly, and said, "Beloved,
    Shall not thy lips give orders to my heart?
Yet there is one small matter in these hills
    Claiming attention ere I can depart.

"Let us not waste these days; thine absent lord
    Cannot return, thou know'st, before the snow

Has melted, and the almond fruits appear."
    This time she answered, "Naught but thee I know!"

I too was young; I could have loved her well
    When her soft eyes across the twilight burned;
But suddenly, around her amber neck,
    The golden beads would sparkle as she turned.

And I remembered; swift mine eyelids fell
    To hide the hate that festered in my soul,
Ever more deeply, with the rising fear
    That Love might wrench Revenge from my control.

But when at last she, acquiescent, lay
    In the sweet-scented shadow of the firs,
Lovely and broken, granting—asking—all,
    It was *his* eyes I met: not hers—not hers!

         *   *   *

Three months I waited: all the village talked,
    And ever anxiously she urged our flight.
Yet still I lingered, till her beauty paled,
    And wearily she came to me at night.

Then, seeing Love, subservient to Revenge,
    Had well achieved his own creative end,
And in his work must soon be manifest,
    Compassing thus my duty to my friend,

One tranquil, sultry night I rode away
   Till far behind the purple hills were dim,
Exulting in my spirit, "Thus I leave
   Her to her fate, and my revenge to him!"

Swiftly he struck her, her lord; the body lay
   With hacked-off breasts, dishonoured, in the Pass.
Months later, riding lonely through the gorge,
   I saw it still, among the long-grown grass.

It was well done; my soul is satisfied.
   Friendship is sweet, and Love is sweeter still,
But Vengeance has a savour all its own—
   A strange delight—well known to those who kill.

Such was the story Afzul told to me,
   While wood-fires crackled in the evening breeze,
And blows on hammered tent-pegs stirred the air
   Sweet with the fragrance from the Sinjib trees.

Tent-like, above, up-held by jagged peaks,
   The heavy purple of the tranquil sky
Shed its oft-broken promises of peace,
   While twinkling stars bemocked the worn-out lie!

Nay, Not To-night

Nay, not to-night;—the slow, sad rain is falling,
  Sorrowful tears, beneath a grieving sky,
Far off a famished jackal, faintly calling,
  Renders the dusk more lonely with its cry.

The mighty river rushes, sobbing, seawards,
  The shadows shelter faint mysterious fears,
I turn mine eyes for consolation theewards,
  And find thy lashes tremulous with tears.

If some new soul, asearch for incarnation,
  Should, through our kisses, enter Life again,
It would inherit all our desolation,
  All the soft sorrow of the slanting rain.

When thou desirest Love's supreme surrender,
  Come while the morning revels in the light,
Bulbuls around us, passionately tender,
  Singing among the roses red and white.

Thus, if it be my sweet and sacred duty,
  Subservient to the Gods' divine decree,

To give the world again thy vivid beauty,
  I should transmit it with my joy in thee.

I could not if I would, Beloved, deceive thee.
  Wouldst thou not feel at once a feigned caress?
Yet, do not rise, I would not have thee leave me,
  My soul needs thine to share its loneliness.

Let the dim starlight, when the low clouds sunder,
  Silver the perfect outline of thy face.
Such faces had the saints; I only wonder
  That thine has sought my heart for resting-place.

The Dying Prince

THERE are no days for me any more, for the dawn is dark with tears,
There is no rest for me any more, for the night is thick with fears,
There are no flowers nor any fruit, for the sorrowful locusts came,
And the garden is but a memory, the vineyard only a name.

There is no light in the empty sky, no sail upon the sea,
Birds are yet on their nests perchance, but they sing no more to me.
Past—vanished—faded away—all the joys that were.
My youth died down in a swift decline when they married her to despair.

"My lord, the crowd in the Audience Hall; how long wilt thou have them wait?"
I have given my father's younger son the guidance of the State.
"The steeds are saddled, the Captains call for the orders of the day."
Tell them that I shall ride no more to the hunting or the fray.

"Sweet the scent of the Moghra flowers"; Brother, it may be so.
"The young, flushed spring is with us again." Is it? I did not know.
"The Zamorin's daughter draweth near, on slender golden feet";
Oh, a curse upon all sweet things say I, to whom they are no more sweet!

Dost think that a man as sick as I can compass a woman's ease?
That the sons of a man who is like to me could ever find rest or peace?
Tell them to marry them where they will, if their longing be so sore,
Such are the things that all men seek, but I shall seek no more.

All my muscles are fallen in, and the blood deserts my veins,
Every fibre and bone of me is waxen full of pains,
The iron feet of mine enemy's curse are heavy upon my head,
Look at me and judge for thyself, thou seest I am but dead.

"Then, who is it, Prince, who has done this thing, has sown such a bitter seed,
That we hale him forth to the Market-place, bind him and let him bleed,

That the flesh may shudder and wince and writhe, redden-
ing 'neath the rod."
Love is the evil-doer, alas! and how shalt thou scourge a
God?

The Hut

Dear little Hut by the rice-fields circled,
    That cocoa-nuts shade above.
I hear the voices of children singing,
    And that means love.

When shall the traveller's march be over,
    When shall his wandering cease?
This little homestead is bare and simple,
    And that means peace.

Nay! to the road I am not unfaithful;
    In tents let my dwelling be!
I am not longing for Peace or Passion
    From any one else but thee,
        My Krishna,
    Any one else but thee!

My Paramour Was Loneliness

My paramour was loneliness
  And lying by the sea,
Soft songs of sorrow and distress
  He did beget in me.

Later another lover came
  More meet for my desire,
"Radiant Beauty" was his name;
  His sons had wings of fire!

The Rice Was Under Water

The Rice was under water, and the land was scourged with rain,
The nights were desolation, and the day was born in pain.
Ah, the famine and the fever and the cruel, swollen streams,
I had died, except for Krishna, who consoled me—in my dreams!

The Burning-Ghats were smoking, and the jewels melted down,
The Temples lay deserted, for the people left the town.
Yet I was more than happy, though passing strange it seems,
For I spent my nights with Krishna, who loved me—in my dreams!

"Surface Rights"

Drifting, drifting down the River,
    Tawny current and foam-flecked tide,
Sorrowful songs of lonely boatmen,
    Mournful forests on either side.

Thine are the outcrops' glittering blocks,
    The quartz where the rich pyrites gleam,
The golden treasure of unhewn rocks
    And the loose gold in the stream.

But,—the dim vast forests along the shore,
    That whisper wonderful things o' nights,—
These are things that I value more,
    My beautiful "surface rights."

Drifting, drifting down the River,—
    Stars a-tremble about the sky—
Ah, my lover, my heart is breaking,
    Breaking, breaking, I know not why.

Why is Love such a sorrowful thing?
    This I never could understand;

Pain and passion are linked together,
  Ever I find them hand in hand.

Loose thy hair in its soft profusion,
  Let thy lashes caress thy cheek,—
These are the things that express thy spirit,
  What is the need to explain or speak?

Drifting, drifting along the River,
  Under the light of a wan low moon,
Steady, the paddles; Boatmen, steady,—
  Why should we reach the sea so soon?

See where the low spit cuts the water,
  What is that misty wavering light?
Only the pale datura flowers
  Blossoming through the silent night.

What is the fragrance in thy tresses?
  'T is the scent of the champa's breath;
The meaning of champa bloom is passion—
  And of datura—death!

Sweet are thy ways and thy strange caresses,
  That sear as flame, and exult as wine.
But I care only for that wild moment
  When my soul arises and reaches thine.

Wistful voices of wild birds calling—
  Far, faint lightning towards the West,—

Twinkling lights of a Tyah homestead,—
  Ruddy glow on a girl's bare breast—

Drifting boats on a mournful River,
  Shifting thoughts in a dreaming mind,—
We two, seeking the Sea, together,—
  When we reach it,—what shall we find?

Shivratri (the Night of Shiva)
(While the procession passed at Ramesram)

Nearer and nearer cometh the car
    Where the Golden Goddess towers,
Sweeter and sweeter grows the air
    From a thousand trampled flowers.
We two rest in the Temple shade
    Safe from the pilgrim flood,
This path of the Gods in olden days
    Ran royally red with blood.

Louder and louder and louder yet
    Throbs the sorrowful drum—
That is the tortured world's despair,
    Never a moment dumb.
Shriller and shriller shriek the flutes,
    Nature's passionate need—
Paler and paler grow my lips,
    And still thou bid'st them bleed.

Deeper and deeper and deeper still,
    Never a pause for pain—

Darker and darker falls the night
    That golden torches stain.
Closer, ah! closer, and still more close,
    Till thy soul reach my soul—
Further, further, out on the tide
    From the shores of self-control.

Glowing, glowing, to whitest heat,
    Thy feverish passions burn,
Fiercer and fiercer, cruelly fierce,
    To thee my senses yearn.
Fainter and fainter runs my blood
    With desperate fight for breath—
This, my Beloved, thou sayest is Love,
    Or I should have deemed it Death!

The First Wife

Ah, my lord, are the tidings true,
That thy mother's jewels are shapen anew?

I hear that a bride has chosen been,
The stars consulted, the parents seen.

Had I been childless, had never there smiled
The brilliant eyes from the face of a child,

Then at least I had understood
This thing they tell me thou findest good.

But I have been down to the River of Death,
With painful footsteps and shuddering breath,

Seven times; thou hast daughters three,
And four young sons who are fair as thee.

I am not unlovely, over my head
Not twenty summers as yet have sped.

'T is eleven years since my opening life
Was given to thee by my father's wife.

Ah, those days—they were lovely to me,
When little and shy I waited for thee.

Till I locked my arms round my lover above,
A child in form but a woman in love.

And I bore thy sons, as a woman should,
Year by year, as is meet and good.

Thy mother was ever content with me—
And oh, Beloved, I worshipped thee!

And now it's over; alas, my lord,
Better I felt thy sharpest sword.

I hear she is youthful and fair as I
When I came to thee in the days gone by.

Her breasts are firmer; this bosom slips
Somewhat, weighted by children's lips.

But they were thy children. Oh, lord my king.
Ah, why hast thy heart devised this thing?

I am not as the women of this thy land,
Meek and timid, broken to hand.

From the distant North I was given to thee,
Whose daughters are passionate, fierce and free.

I could not dwell by a rival's side,
I seek a bridegroom, as thou a bride.

The night she yieldeth her youth to thee,
Death shall take his pleasure in me.

I Arise and Go Down to the River

I ARISE and go down to the River, and currents that come
    from the sea,
Still fresh with the salt of the ocean, are lovely and precious
    to me,
The waters are silver and silent, except where the kingfisher
    dips,
Or the ripples wash off from my shoulder the reddening stain
    of thy lips.

Two things make my joy at this moment: thy gold-coloured
    beauty by night,
And the delicate charm of the River, all pale in the day-
    breaking light,
So cool are the waters' caresses. Ah, which is the lovelier,—
    this?
Or the fire that it kindles at midnight, beneath the soft glow
    of thy kiss?

Ah, Love has a mighty dominion, he forges with passionate
    breath
The links which stretch out to the Future, with forces of life
    and of death,

1 Arise and Go Down to the River

But great is the charm of the River, so soft is the sigh of the
  reeds,
They give me, long sleepless from passion, the peace that my
  weariness needs.
I float on the breast of my River, and startle the birds on the
  edge,
To land on a newly found island, a boat that is caught in the
  sedge,
The rays of the sun are still level, not yet has the heat of the
  day
Deflowered the mists of the morning, that linger in delicate
  grey.

What land was his dwelling whose fancy first gave unto Par-
  adise birth?
He never had swum in my River, or else he had fixed it on
  earth!
Oh, grace of the palm-tree reflections, oh, sense of the wind
  from the sea!
Oh, divine and serene exultation of one who is lonely and
  free!

Ah, delicate breezes of daybreak, so scentless, refreshing and
  free!
And yet—had my midnight been lonely you had been less
  lovely to me.
This coolness comes laden with solace, because I am hot from
  the fire,
As often devotion to virtue arises from sated desire.

Gautama came forth from his Palace; he felt the night wind on his face,
He loathed, as he left, the embraces, the softness and scent of the place,
But, ah, if his night had been loveless, with no one to solace his need,
He never had written that sermon which men so devotedly read.

Ah, River, thy gentle persuasion; I doubt if I seek any more
The beauty that hurts me and holds me beneath the low roof on the shore.
I loved thee, ay, loved—for a season, but thou, was it love or desire,
The glow of the Sun in his glory, or only the heat of a fire?

I think not that thou wilt regret me, for thou art too joyous and fair,
So many are keen to caress thee, thy passionate midnights to share.
Thou wilt not have time to remember, before a new love-knot is tied,
The stranger who loved thee and left thee, who drifted away on the tide.

Two things I have found that are lovely, though most things are sullen and grey;
One: Peace—but what mortal has found him; and Passion—but when would he stay?

So I shall return to my River, and floating at ease on its breast,
Shall find, what Love never has given—a sense of most infinite rest.

When the years have gone by and departed, what thought shall I keep of this land?
A curl of thy waist-reaching tresses? a flower received from thy hand?
Nay, if I can fathom the future, I fancy my relic will be
Some shell, my beloved one, the River has stol'n from the store of the sea.

Listen, Beloved

Listen, Beloved, the Casurinas quiver,
  Each tassel prays the wind to set it free,
Hark to the frantic sobbing of the river,
  Wild to attain extinction in the sea.
All Nature blindly struggles to dissolve
In other forms and forces, thus to solve
The painful riddle of identity.
Ah, that my soul might lose itself in thee!

Yet, my Beloved One, wherefore seek I union,
  Since there is no such thing in all the world,—
Are not our spirits linked in close communion,—
  And on my lips thy clinging lips are curled?
Thy tender arms are round my shoulders thrown,
I hear thy heart more loudly than my own,
And yet, to my despair, I know thee far,
As in the stellar darkness, star from star.

Even in times when love with bounteous measure
  A simultaneous joy on us has shed,
In the last moment of delirious pleasure,
  Ere the sense fail, or any force be fled,

My rapture has been even as a wall,
Shutting out any thought of thee at all!
My being, by its own delight possessed,
Forgot that it was sleeping on thy breast.

Ay, from his birth each man is vowed and given
    To a vast loneliness, ungauged, unspanned,
Whether by pain and woe his soul be riven,
    Or all fair pleasures clustered 'neath his hand.
His gain by day, his ecstasy by night,—
His force, his folly, fierce or faint delight,—
Suffering or sorrow, fortune, feud, or care,—
Whate'er he find or feel,—he may not share.

Lonely we join the world, and we depart
    Even as lonely, having lived alone,
The breast that feeds us, the beloved one's heart,
    The lips we kiss,—or curse—alike unknown.
Ay, even these lips of thine, so often kissed,
What certitude have I that they exist?
Alas, it is the truth, though harsh it seems,
I have been loved as sweetly in my dreams.

Therefore if I should seem too fiercely fond,
    Too swift to love, too eager to attain,
Forgive the fervour that would forage beyond
    The limits set to mortal joy and pain.
Knowing the soul's unmeasured loneliness,

My passion must be mingled with distress,
As I, despairing, struggle to draw near
What is as unattainable as dear.

Thirst may be quenched at any kindly river,
   Rest may be found 'neath any arching tree.
No sleep allures, no draughts of love deliver
   My spirit from its aching need of thee.
Thy sweet assentiveness to my demands,
All the caressive touches of thy hands,—
These soft cool hands, with fingers tipped with fire,—
They can do nothing to assuage desire.

Sometimes I think my longing soul remembers
   A previous love to which it aims and strives,
As if this fire of ours were but the embers
   Of some wild flame burnt out in former lives.
Perchance in earlier days I *did* attain
That which I seek for now so all in vain,
Maybe my soul with thine *was* fused and wed
In some great night, long since dissolved and dead.

We may progress; but who shall answer clearly
   The riddle of the endless change of things.
Perchance in other days men loved more dearly,
   Or Love himself had wider ways and wings,
Maybe we gave ourselves with less control,
Or simpler living left more free the soul,

So that with ease the flesh aside was flung,—
Or was it merely that *Mankind was young?*

Or has my spirit a divine prevision
    Of vast vague passions stored in days to be,
When some strong souls shall conquer their division
    And two shall be as one, eternally?
Finding at last upon each other's breast,
Unutterable calm and infinite rest,
While love shall burn with so intense a glow
That both shall die, and neither heed or know.

Why do I question thus, and wake confusion
    In the soft thought that lights thy perfect face,
Ah, shed once more thy perfumed hair's profusion,
    Open thine arms and make my resting place.
Lay thy red lips on mine as heretofore,
Grant me the treasure of thy beauty's store,
Stifle all thought in one imperious kiss,—
What shall I ask for more than this,— and this?

Oh, Unforgotten and Only Lover

Oh, unforgotten and only lover,
   Many years have swept us apart,
But none of the long dividing seasons
   Slay your memory in my heart.
In the clash and clamour of things unlovely
   My thoughts drift back to the times that were,
When I, possessing thy pale perfection,
   Kissed the eyes and caressed the hair.

Other passions and loves have drifted
   Over this wandering, restless soul,
Rudderless, chartless, floating always
   With some new current of chance control.
But thine image is clear in the whirling waters—
   Ah, forgive—that I drag it there,
For it is so part of my very being
   That where I wander it too must fare.

Ah, I have given thee strange companions,
   To thee—so slender and chaste and cool—
But a white star loses no glimmer of beauty
   In all the mud of a miry pool

'That holds the grace of its white reflection;
  Nothing could fleck thee, nothing could stain,
Thou hast made a home for thy delicate beauty
  Where all things peaceful and lovely reign.

Doubtless the night that my soul remembers
  Was a sin to thee, and thine only one.
Thou thinkest of it, if thou thinkest ever,
  As a crime committed, a deed ill done.
But for me, the broken, the desert-dweller,
  Following Life through its underways,—
I know if those midnights thou hadst not granted
  I had not lived through these after days.

And that had been well for me; all would say so,
  What have I done since I parted from thee?
But things that are wasted, and full of ruin,
  All unworthy, even of me.
Yet, it was to me that the gift was given,
  No greater joy have the Gods above,—
That night of nights when my only lover,
  Though all reluctant, granted me love.

For thy beauty was mine, and my spirit knows it,
  Never, ah, never my heart forgets,
One thing fixed, in the torrent of changing,
  Faults and follies and fierce regrets.
Thine eyes and thy hair, that were lovely symbols
  Of that white soul that their grace enshrined,

They are part of me and my life for ever,
   In every fibre and cell entwined.

Men might argue that having known thee
   I had grown faithful and pure as thee,
Had turned at the touch of thy grace and glory
   From the average pathways trodden by me.
Hadst thou been kinder or I been stronger
   It may be even these things had been—
But one thing is clear to my soul for ever,
   I owe my owning of thee to sin.

Had I been colder I had not reached thee,
   Besmirched the ermine, beflecked the snow—
It was only sheer and desperate passion
   That won thy beauty in years ago.
And not for the highest virtues in Heaven,
   The utmost grace that the soul can name,
Would I resign what the sin has brought me,
   Which I hold glory, and thou—thy shame.

I talk of sin in the usual fashion,
   But God knows what is a sin to me—
We love more fiercely or love more faintly—
   But I doubt if it matters how these things be.
The best and the worst of us all sink under—
   What I held passion and thou held'st lust—
What name will it find in a few more seasons,
   When we both dissolve in an equal dust?

If a God there be, and a God seems needed
   To make the beauty of things like thee,
He doubtless also, some careless moment,
   Mixed the forces that fashioned me.
Also He, for His own good reason—
   Though I care little how these things are—
Gave me thee, in those few brief midnights,
   And that one solace He never can mar.

Ah me, the stars of such varying heavens
   Have watched me, under such alien skies,
Lay thy beauty naked before me
   To soothe and solace my world-worn eyes.
For one good gift to me has been given—
   A memory accurate, clear and keen,
That holds the vision, perfect for ever
   In charm and glory, of things once seen.

So I hold thee there, and my fancy wanders
   To each known beauty and blue-veined place,
I know how each separate eyelash trembles,
   And every shadow that sweeps thy face.
And this is a joy of which none can rob me,
   This is a pleasure that none can mar—
As sweet as thou wert, in that long past midnight,
   Even as lovely my memories are.

Ah, unforgotten and only lover,
   If ever I drift across thy thought,

As even a vision unloved, unlovely,
  May cross the fancy, uncalled, unsought,
When the years that pass thee have shown, in passing,
  That my love, *in its strength at least*, was rare—
Wilt thou not think—ah, hope of the hopeless—
  E'en as thou wouldst not, thou wilt not—care!

Early Love

Who says I wrong thee, my half-opened rose?
Little he knows of thee or me, or love.—
I am so tender of thy fragile youth,
Yea, in my hours of wildest ecstasy,
Keeping close-bitted each careering sense.
Only I give mine eyes unmeasured law
To feed them where they will, and *their* delight
Was curbed at first, until thy tender shame
Died in the bearing of thy first born joy.

I am not cruel, my half-opened rose,
Though in the sunshine of my own desire
I have uncurled thy petals to the light
And fed the tendrils of thy dawning sense
With delicate caresses, till they leave
Thee tremulous with the newness of thy joy,
Sharing thy lover's fire with innocent flame.

Others will wrong thee, that I well foresee,
Being a man, knowing my fellow men,
And they who, knowing, would blame my love of thee
Contentedly will see thy beauty given,

When the world judges thou art ripe to wed,—
To the rough rites of marriage, to the pain
And grievous weariness of child-getting.—
This shall be right and licit in their eyes—
But it would break my heart, were I alive.

Yea, this will be; many will doubtless share
The rose whose bud has been my one delight,
And I shall not be there to shield my flower.
Yet, I have taught thee of the ways of men,
Much I have learnt in cities and in courts,
Winnowed to suit thy tender brain,—is thine,
Thus Life shall find thee, not all unprepared
To face its callous, subtle cruelties.

Still,—it will profit little; I discern
Thou art of those whose love will prove their curse,
—Thou sayest thou lovest me, to thy delight?
Nay, little one, it is not love as yet.
Dear as thou art, and lovely, thou canst not love,
Thy later loves shall show the truth of this.

Ay, by some subtle signs I know full well
That thou art capable of that great love
Whose glory has the light of unknown heavens,
And makes hot Hell for those who harbour it.

Naught I can say could save thee from thyself,
Ah, were I half my age! Yet even that,

Had been too old for thy sweet thirteenth year.
Still, thou art happy now, and glad thine eyes,
When, as the lilac evening gains the sky,
I lay thee, 'twixt thine own soft hair and me,
Kissing thy senses into soft delight.
Ruffling the petals of my half-closed rose
With tender touches, and perpetual care
That no wild moment of mine own delight
Deep in the flower's heart,—should set the fruit.

Ah, in the days to come, it well may be,
When thou shalt see thy beauty stained and torn
By the harsh sequel of some future love,
Thy thoughts shall stray to thy first lover's grave,
And thou shalt murmur, "Ay, but that was love.
They were most wrong who said he did me wrong.
Only I was too young to understand."

Vayu the Wind

Ah, Wind, I have always loved thee
    Since those far off nights
When I lay beneath the vines
    A prey to strange delights,
For among my tresses
Thy soft caresses
    Were sweet as a lover's to me.

Later thou grewest more wanton, or I more shy,
And after the bath I drew my garments close,
Fearing thy soft persuasion amongst my hair,
When thou camest fresh with the scent of some ruffled rose.

Ah, Wind, thou hast lain with the Desert,
    I know her savour well,
  And the spices wherewith she scents her breasts—
She who has known such countless lovers
Yet rarely borne a city among her sands—
    Thou comest as one from a night of love,
      Thy breath is broken and hard,—
  Bringing echoes of lonely things,
      Vast and cruel, that the soft and golden sands
      Buried beneath thin ripples so long ago.

Ah, Wind, thou hast given me lovely things,
    The scent of a thousand flowers,
And the heavy perfume of pollen-laden fields,
Strange snatches of wild song from the heart of the dark
                                          Bazaar
    That thrilled to my very core,
Till I threw the sheet aside and rose to follow,—
    But whither, or what?

Also, Wind, thou broughtest the breath of the sea,
    The sound of its myriad waves.
And in nights when I lay on the lonely sands
    Stretching mine arms to thee,
    Thou gavest me something—faint and vast and sweet,
Something ineffable, wistful, from far away,
        Elsewhere—Beyond—

And thou wast kind to me in my times of love,
        Cooling my lips
    That my lover wore away,
While, wafting the scent from his divided hair,
    Thou show'dst the stars between
Far away, and eclipsed by his burning eyes
        Even the stars.

And now I almost foresee the place and the hour
    When I shall open my dying lips to thee
        And receive a last cool kiss.

Afterwards, Wind, since I have always loved thee,—
    Whirl my dust to the scented heart of a moghra flower,
      His flower, but, ah, thou knowest,—
    So often thy kisses have mingled with his and mine.

www.ingramcontent.com/pod-product-compliance
Lightning Source LLC
Chambersburg PA
CBHW032028150426
43194CB00006B/192